'My Yorkshireness owes much to Grannie,' says the author of this magical book, recently retired from editorship of *The Dalesman*, the worldfamous magazine with which he has been associated for more than forty years. At the age of 94, Grannie lived alone at Bradley, in a side-valley of the Aire, spry and vigorous, her speech a treasury of dialect words and expressions. Grannie knew nothing of the world beyond the Dales but what she had seen from the high moors in her youth. She was typical of her generation, and typical of the wonderful, memorable characters which people this book.

W. R. MITCHELL

A Dalesman's Diary

A Futura Book

First published in Great Britain by Souvenir Press Ltd
and simultaneously in Canada in 1989
This Futura edition published in 1990

Copyright © 1989 by W. R. Mitchell

ISBN 0 7088 4750 1

Reproduced, printed and bound in Great Britain by
BPCC Hazell Books
Aylesbury, Bucks, England
Member of BPCC Ltd.

Futura Publications
A Division of
Macdonald & Co (Publishers) Ltd
Orbit House
1 New Fetter Lane
London EC4A 1AR
A member of Maxwell Macmillan Pergamon Publishing Corporation

Contents

Contents

Chapter 1

A Yorkshire Upbringing

My Yorkshireness owes much to Grannie, who lived at Bradley, in a little side-valley of the Aire. She was incredibly old—small, bent, and as wrinkled as a prune that has not yet been steeped in water. At tea-time I watched, enthralled, as beetroot juice from the salad trickled along the minute gutters in the skin around her mouth. She lived alone, at the age of 94, passing her days pleasantly with housework, and using the Primitive Methodist Chapel as her spiritual home and social centre. There was 'summat going on at t'Chapil' nearly every day of the week.

Grannie had been a Miss Gill from Lane Top when she married Grandad. She was 'as Yorksher as they mak 'em', her speech made vivid by a treasury of dialect words and expressions. When the house was untidy, it was 'all of a scrow'. This was never the case on Sunday, of course, a flurry of housework ensuring that the living room was Sabbath-bright. Her last tasks before going to bed were to cover the table with a rich red cloth fringed by tassles, and to place on the table an open Bible, the *Christian Herald* and a magnifying glass.

Grannie could never understand why her eyesight was not as keen as it had been, though it was good enough, with the aid of some handed-down spectacles, to maintain her independence; she also made 'pegged' rugs by the dozen.

My father and I always called to see her at blackberry time. No larger, more succulent berries could be found than those which grew against the sandstone rocks in disused quarries around the village of Bradley. We offered her a share of the purple harvest. She always shook her head sadly and remarked, 'Nay, t'seeds get under me teeth.'

Grannie's first name was Selina. All her family had been named after Biblical characters, including Hobadiah— invariably referred to as 'Our 'Ob'. Her memory of the outer world was restricted to what she had seen from the high moors in her young days, though she had been on a Chapel choir trip to Morecambe. She passed her old age quietly, while the pot-dogs looked down from the high mantelpiece and the kettle on the open fire had a continuous song in its heart.

I do not remember much about Grandfather, except that he was a Socialist of the old-fashioned sort, and that Margaret Bonfield, a Labour pioneer, once came to tea. Primitive Methodists and Wesleyan Methodists did not mix religiously: there was no love lost between Grandfather (a Prim) and the local mill-owner ('one of t'other lot') over union matters. A disagreement about wage levels led to Grandfather being sacked on the spot. Henceforth, he had to walk six miles to and from work in a mill at Skipton. He contrived to establish a weavers' union, to take services as a local preacher and to teach in Sunday School. When I last saw him he lay in his coffin in the spare bedroom. The mirror had been turned: it was unlucky to view a corpse through a looking-glass.

Those days were dedicated to hard wark (work) with no scrattin' about (being aimless). The Devil had jobs for idle hands, we were taught. In due course, the 'warkers' died, many of them prematurely through overwork. Grannie's folk were among those buried in the cemetery on the hillside. I thought it was a pity they could not continue to appreciate the view—a vista of dale and moor, held together by miles of drystone walls.

Father had many a graveyard tale to relate. This was not morbidity but the Methodist lack of fear about death which, we were taught, was just another beginning. Father would take me to a tombstone of one of the Gills. Inscribed thereon was the word 'Resting'. It seems that in life Mr Gill was shiftless (lazy). He never did owt else but rest!

A woman who lost her husband had the words 'Rest in Peace' inscribed on the tombstone. When she began to hear 'things' about him and other women, she arranged for the monumental mason to add '. . . Till I Come'. I heard of the old couple who walked away from a graveside, having 'buried' their 60-year-old son. The man said to his wife: 'I telled thee we wouldn't rear 'im.'

As Father and I crossed the moors between Skipton and Bradley, to visit Grannie, we would stop where ice-cold water gurgled from the gritstone. While serving in the Navy during the 1914–18 war, Father had lain delirious in hospital in Salonika, thinking ot the moorland well and vowing that if he was 'spared' he would make a pilgrimage to it and sip the water. This he did—again and again.

I enjoyed those moorland days. We heard the crowing of the red grouse—'kowack, kowack'—and found some precocious chicks. A ring ouzel perched on a gritstone outcrop chacked its displeasure, flaunting its white 'bib' before vanishing into a mini-jungle of bracken at the edge of the gill. Larks rose like feathered helicopters. The air shivered with the trilling of curlews. Stored on the sensitive colour film of my mind are early impressions of curlews perched on the capstones of walls or undertaking their song-glides, bringing life back to the uplands where, in winter, we heard little more than the coarse honking of the carrion crow.

From the edge of the moors, we looked northwards to where Sharphaw lay like a huge brown bell tent, pitched just beyond Skipton. We saw the oxbows of the Aire, silvery in sunshine, between unspoilt water-meadows. One of the two becks that form the Aire, up by Malham, had inspired Charles Kingsley when thinking about *The Water-Babies*. As a special treat, we might go to Bolton Abbey, which now is a ten-minute car journey from town and then seemed half a world away. I saw where the Wharfe, in the early manhood of its life, was pent in by gritstone rocks at the Strid. The water swirled darkly and

grim tales were told of reckless people who, while attempting to leap across, fell in, their bodies becoming lodged in
subterranean crevices!

George Green, who owned the mill—and once sacked
Grandfather!—regularly invited William Riley, author of
the novel *Windyridge*, to take services at 'the top chapel' in
Bradley. Mr Riley had written lots of books, it was said. He
mentioned in one address the lonely dales that lay far to the
north, dales drained by the rivers Tees and Swale. Grannie
distinguished between them 'at preyches (preaches) and
them 'at teaches, preferring the former. Nevertheless, she
enjoyed listening to William Riley; his visit was counted as
a special day. I was awestruck by the thought of anyone
coming to quiet little Bradley from B-r-a-d-f-o-r-d. The
Mitchells marked the occasion by a family gathering and the
opening of tinned salmon—then a great luxury, especially
if it had not been mixed with breadcrumbs for economy.

Grannie fell and broke a leg. She recovered and said,
brightly, 'If owt else 'appens to me, thou mun shoot me!'
She fell again, was taken to hospital and—grieved herself
into the grave.

In Mother's family, the Cartmans, there was a measure of
pride in the fact that old Dr Cartman had been a personal
friend of Patrick Brontë, the parson at Haworth. The good
doctor moved to Skipton from Bingley on his appointment
as Headmaster of Ermysted's Grammar School. One of his
sons, my grandfather, was obsessed with cricket and
angling. Another son played the odd cricket match for
Yorkshire, but couldn't get on with Lord Hawke! Grandfather's fishing water was not some expensive salmon
reach but the murky, somewhat smelly water of the Leeds
and Liverpool canal.

If Grandfather did not turn up for a cricket match at
Skipton, someone ran along t'Cut bank to locate him. His
waterway was periodically stirred up by barges laden with
coal for Dewhurst's mill. Any coal that fell from a barge was
scooped up by a shirtless entrepreneur, one Billy Gelling,
using a long pole and bucket into which holes had been

punched. He sold the coal about town at a bargain price. The red-brick chimney of Dewhurst's mill lacerated the passing clouds and provided Skipton with the equivalent of an exclamation mark.

Our Skipton Grannie was the spit-and-image of Queen Victoria, being small, dumpy, clad in black and with something of a regal appearance when seated. Skipton was half full of dumpy little ladies who had produced large families quickly. This God-fearing Grannie had one minor weakness: playing the card game Newmarket for halfpennies on a Sunday evening. I would see her, with two or three relatives or friends, gathered round a table, the drawers of which had been left half-open in case the Rector turned up unexpectedly. He never did.

Skipton prided itself on its status of 'gateway to the Dales'. A small compact town, it lies in the Aire Gap, where the Pennine Chain, stretching for 250 miles from Derbyshire into Scotland, has a missing link. Skipton is on the border between a great industrial belt and the largely unspoilt Dales country in which there was scarcely a mill chimney to be seen before Carlisle was reached. I spent many hours before a railway poster at the station; the picture showed Carlisle as gateway to Scotland, with a mounted knight in attendance. Skipton had its dash of romance in the Norman castle, its newer gateway flanked by drum towers and surmounted by huge letters in stone —DES OR MAIS, or 'Henceforward', the motto of the fabulous Cliffords. In the parish church were Clifford tombs, emblazoned with coats of arms, also an inconspicuous piece of stained glass, with the initials AP, for Anne Pembroke, otherwise known as Lady Anne Clifford. She died in 1676, but her spirit lived on at Skipton where old folk spoke of her as though she had just 'passed on'. As a small child, I heard so much about Lady Anne I began to think of her as one of my aunties.

Skipton, an ancient market town, served the West Riding dales, as far as the head of Wharfedale. It had also become part of the domain of King Cotton, who extended his territory from Lancashire by way of the Aire Gap. When trade was good, the town vibrated with the power of rows of Lancashire looms, driven from Lancashire boilers by way of miles of leather-belting which swayed between drive-shafts and machines in misty weaving sheds. The mills poured warm, stale water into Eller Beck ('the stream of the fairies'), which delivered it to the Aire. In bad times, the air cleared of smoke and the mill-people clammed (went hungry). The kingfisher still flew like a blue dart behind Skipton Castle, which overlooked the Springs Canal, and also along the Aire, where it subsisted on pollution-tolerant minnows.

On market days, I saw farm folk in town. The men wore cloth caps, tweedy coats, smart trousers with shiny leggings and their best setting-off boots, agleam with much polishing. In those straitened times, many arrived by bus or train; few families had cars. A farmer from West Craven —somebody's Uncle Wallace—caused a sensation when he arrived in town in a yellow-sided car. Farmers' wives carried baskets containing butter and eggs.

The dalesfolk had a strange, clipped tongue. The keyword was 'Aye', uttered with subtle changes to the pitch and modulation. The basic conversation was, 'Owt?' to which the reply was, 'Nowt.' A garrulous man might observe, 'How's t'wife?' Reply: 'Aw reet' or 'Nobbut middlin'.' The weather was bound to come into a conversation. 'Does ta think it'll rain?' someone would say, prompting a doleful reply, ''Appen.'

* * *

My Yorkshireness was confirmed at school. I became familiar with the map of the county and was intrigued by the curious wiggles of its boundary, which gave Lancashire a waist like a wasp and poked a finger of land up to Mickle Fell, tickling the ribs of Old Westmorland. I was taught that Yorkshire was so vast it had to be split into Ridings, or thirdings, and how—if you thought of a hand—the central plain of Yorkshire was the palm and the Dales the fingers, extending into the high hills, those bleak hills which the

Norse settlers of old had called 'fells'. I began to explore the Dales and to read more about them. I discovered that between the valleys of Tees, Swale, Ure, Wharfe, Aire and Nidd lay vast areas of high country, and that in a score of places the hills overtopped the 2,000 foot contour.

I ventured on to upland plateaux which in early summer were whitened by the downy seed heads of cotton grass (actually a sedge). I saw Malham Cove, a cliff of purest limestone gleaming chalk-white against a blue-black storm cloud, yet after evening rain any limestone that caught the eye of the sun was a delicate pink. On dry ridges and across half the landscape to the east, late summer offered the pageant of empurpled heather. It was a good time for all but the grouse, which had to fly through a fusillade of lead. By late autumn, the coppery hue of dying bracken fronds stained many a fellside, except where some thrifty farmers had mown and then carted the bracken to provide winter-time bedding for the stock. With few native trees remaining on the 'tops', the winter landscape could be stark and empty.

A botanist friend of the family showed me rarities like holly fern and promptly placed a piece of limestone over part of a young plant so that it would not be conspicuous to collectors. He suggested I might study geology by looking at the drystone walls. 'You can bet your life a good waller would not carry his material far!'

Fortunately for me, the Dales geology is fairly simple —carboniferous, with the beds tilting towards the east and showing a succession of rocks like layers in a sandwich cake: Great Scar Limestone; the Yoredale Series (bands of limestone, shales and sandstones, lying above the Great Scar Limestone); and Millstone Grit (so named because this coarse material was ideal for grindstones as it did not overheat the grain). The first vivid impressions remained; the terminology came later.

Slowly, through inquiry, reading and the enthusiasm of teachers, especially Harry Gill, I became aware of immense changes that had occurred in my home district. Drainage made the first cuts into the ancient plateau and much later the water-eroded valleys felt the abrasive ice sheets of the Pleistocene period. Glaciers broadened and deepened the valleys, depositing on their sides the porridge-like mush we know as boulder clay. There were calm, temperate, inter-glacial periods (such as today). In distant times, woolly rhinocerous and hyena were among the local fauna, as revealed by their remains, taken from limestone caves in the Settle district.

About 10,000 years ago—a mere blink in the story of the landscape—the dales themselves were in a form we would now recognise, except that lakes occupied many of the valleys and trees had become established on all but the highest ground. The first men fished in the lakes and hunted wild animals. A slash-and-burn policy, followed by the grazing of many sheep, prevented natural regeneration of much of the timber, leading to leaching of minerals and the impoverished state of the Dales landscape today.

If you see an isolated tree on a hillside, it is more than likely that it is growing from a pothole, or from the side of a cliff where it has rooted beyond the reach of the ubiquitous sheep. Overstocking with sheep debased many a hill, leading to the disappearance of heather from the drier ridges and to the formation of vistas dominated by mat grass.

My schooling extended into the war period. For a time we carried gas masks. The mill buzzer warned us when enemy aircraft were around. A highlight of every week was buying spice (sweets), which then were severely rationed. Shop windows held an array of cardboard dummies of the items normally sold. Stocks of cigarettes went 'under the counter' and eventually the only types readily available were those made from tobacco from Egypt or Pakistan.

The governmental call-up into the Forces denuded our town of the fit and young. Some of them returned wearing the bright blue suits of the wounded. Father, having joined the Territorials, being genuinely concerned about the Nazi rise to power, soon found himself with the BEF in France.

Meanwhile, our Methodist parson opened a canteen for the troops and called it 'The Better 'Ole' after one of the 1914–18 war cartoons. The troops came and went.

Prisoners of war arrived at a new redbrick camp beside the Bolton Abbey road, and we became familiar with men on parole, wearing battle-dress with large, colourful patches on their backs. We youngsters heard that these would act as targets to the armed guards if the prisoners decided to run away! One of the prisoners began to attend our Chapel. At Christmas, he asked if he might play the organ. There were some misgivings, but eventually permission was granted. I watched him walk to the organ, flexing fingers which had spent the previous week lifting roots from the fields. He played a line from a carol, then improvised for fifteen minutes.

He accompanied the hymns splendidly, and after the Benediction gave a magnificent rendering of Bach's *Toccata and Fugue*, to an audience who remained seated, having been stunned into silence. The little man in the shabby battle-dress left the organ stool and returned to the vestry, passing a diminutive old lady who said, 'By gum, lad —thou's played afore!' He had—in a cathedral in Germany.

I grew up with Handel's *Messiah* and spent part of every Easter listening to Stainer's *Crucifixion*. I had formed a considerable love for Mendelssohn's *Hebrides Overture*, music which tied up nicely with the old Kearton wildlife books I had borrowed from the library, for the Keartons had taken their cameras and notebooks to the wild west of Scotland. I bought the record, and overcame a major snag —the fact that I had no gramophone—by running errands for dear old Mrs Hurst, who lived opposite and owned one of the finest models. So, each Saturday morning, I was allowed to take my one and only record to her home. For a short time, Mendelssohn held sway, with his musical impression of roaring waves and the cries of seabirds.

It so happened that Mrs Hurst's brother was William Moss and that he was managing director of the Craven

Herald, Ltd., publishers of the local newspaper. Perhaps the Editor knew that, when I applied for a job as a reporter, or perhaps he hired me through desperation, many of his staff having joined the Forces. Or perhaps . . .

Chapter 2

Junior Reporter

It so happened that I followed William Moss into the *Herald* building on my first morning as a reporter, in 1943. The extreme cordiality I experienced was for William, not for me. He was not much to look at; indeed, there was not much of him to see. He was somewhat shabby and carried a carpet-bag. Charles Dickens might have found a place in one of his novels for a man like William Moss.

When he turned to enter the *Craven Herald* shop, I was perhaps four yards behind him. The shop staff wished us 'Good morning'. Not knowing where I should be in the echoing caverns beyond, I simply followed Mr Moss, up the rickety stairs, into an office heated by a coal fire.

With a feeling of unease, I realised I was now part of a procession. Ahead of me was the man I later discovered was the editor/manager, and behind him the corpulent form of the advertisement manager, followed by Mr Moss, a clerk bearing a file—and me. A young woman tittered. A middle-aged woman looked frosty. The advertisement manager was bemused. Swept up in this surge of activity, I found myself in the big front office where, normally, the editor/manager was a solitary figure. William Moss sat at a long table. The file was placed before him by a clerk who, I am sure, walked backwards as he left. The file was opened. An invoice was withdrawn and placed on the table. The advertisement manager handed a black stamp to our distinguished visitor who, with appropriate solemnity, applied it to the invoice. It was borne away, to be delivered to some luckless person who had not paid an account and who, as the weeks had gone by, had received reminders of increasing severity—first yellow, then blue, and now black, with a message threatening legal action if it was not settled immediately.

Eventually I was installed in the Reporter's Room of the *Herald*, among battered furniture and drifts of yellowing newsprint. The door was kicked open by someone who entered with proofs. The door slammed shut behind him through the agency of a heavy lead weight suspended from a length of the type of cord used for parcelling up newspapers. I cannot remember now if the newcomer was Donald or John Henry; they completed the head office reporting staff. Seconds later the door opened again. Into view, moving briskly, came the sub-editor, Harry J. Scott, who lived somewhere up the Dales. He might have said, 'Good morning,' or perhaps, 'Hallo.' Instead, he greeted me with the words, 'Hail to thee, blithe spirit . . .' It marked him out as someone special.

He dumped his attaché case and went clattering down the back stairs to have a chat with the editor, John Mitchell. I was sent to buy some of Mr Bean's pork pies. His shop stood in Middle Row. As I returned, I felt the warmth of the pies against my hand. Back in the office, proof-reading was in progress. I held a mass of 'copy' as someone attempted to read the smudged 6 point type. The voice was a monotone, like a medieval chant, stopping briefly when an error was found and corrected. I chewed at Mr Bean's pork pie and felt the warm gravy dripping between my fingers onto the cracked linoleum.

Harry Scott returned with 'copy' he had collected from the editor. He pressed Tom Long tobacco into the charred bowl of his pipe, puffed vigorously, creating a smoke screen which took minutes to clear, and devoted himself to handing out the copy for attention. In my case, I had the fourth carbon copy of some indifferently written news from a Wharfedale village. Reading it was fractionally more difficult than typing it, using a small portable machine which had only one shift key, or the old standard machine

which sounded like a Lancashire loom. The 'copy' paper
was from the outer layers of the rolls of newsprint—paper
that was already pitted with holes and was further lacerated
by the mechanism of the typewriter. Harry Scott called a
typewriter a 'tripewriter' and claimed that nothing but
literary tripe was produced using a machine.

There would be other memorable events before that first
morning at the *Herald* drew to a close. We heard the
thunder of rapid footfalls on the bare boards of the staircase. Anyone travelling at such a speed must be the bearer
of bad tidings. The door was opened by a farmer from the
head of Wharfedale. He was down for the market and wore
his 'best setting off' clothes. Nonetheless, he had the
cloying, earthy tang of cow-muck, which he had doubtless
been spreading in his fields that very morning. He dis-
pensed with formalities, and declared, 'It's about yon item
in t "Fifty Years Ago" column.'

We produced the item that offended him. He pointed out
an error. We promised to make a correction in the next
issue. It seemed to satisfy him. He stopped near the door,
sighed and remarked, 'I telled 'em about it fifty year ago.'
Would we never learn?

I had been on the staff for four hours when the whole
building echoed to a thwacking sound, like the territorial
'drumming' of some giant woodpecker. 'It's Reg,' said
John. In the temporary absence of Harry Scott, he lifted the
lid of his desk and revealed a poem, neatly typed:

> What is the sound I hear so oft,
> Like wind among the willows—
> Rising and falling, and ever soft?
> Hark, tis the burbling Billows!

Reg Billows, a family friend for many years, was now
revealed as a man who liked to get things done—instantly.
When the first round of thwacking with a rod against the
back of a door was over, a bellow was to be heard. Then
more thwacking, until someone went down to collect some
proofs. If not, Reg would appear in all his ferocity, with

proofs and 'copy' in hand. These he dumped in the lap of the nearest reporter. I had hitherto pictured Reg as the quiet, solitary man who spent his time in a greenhouse or tending gladioli.

At lunchtime I sallied forth into Skipton, conscious of my new role in local society. A pencil protruding from my top pocket scratched my neck. A bulky notebook in my left-hand side pocket was already pulling a good jacket out of shape. I strode up and down the High Street, between Woolworths and the drum-towers flanking the gateway to Skipton Castle. I strode on the long-remembered towpath of the Springs Canal, between Eller Beck and the castle on its immense rock. The route had become familiar to me as a small boy delivering newspapers, a job lasting as long as the patience of the newsagent and his customers. The final straw had been when I set out to deliver magazines one washday when the back streets of the town were a mass of flapping clothing in the course of being dried by a March breeze. The heavy shop-bike had gone out of control on a cobbled hill and I had run it through five rows of washing before bringing it to a halt between a lamp post and a wall.

On the way back to the office, I reflected on my first experience of the workings of the Press. There is Methodism in my madness: much of my spare time was spent at the Chapel, which was then a social centre as well as a place of worship. When the huge room below the Chapel had been redecorated, a celebratory gathering had been planned and the *Herald* invited to send a photographer. Along came Fred, complete with plate camera and flash-powder held aloft in a metal tray and ignited at the precise moment the camera lens was open. Fred had assembled us on the stage. He fine-focused the heavy camera and rested it on a tripod. The tray holding the flash powder was held aloft. There was a whoosh and a terrifying flash of light. For a second or two, I saw Fred standing by his camera, and then we were all enveloped in smoke from the controlled explosion. It was dark, acrid and slow to clear. When normality had returned, a roar of Christian anger might be heard as the chapelgoers noticed the big black mark on the ceiling.

In 1943, I was paid 12s/6d a week for my labours. When I mildly protested, I was told that the last reporter to be hired before the war had paid the management for his training. Newsprint was rationed. Buildings had to be 'blacked out' so that no chink of light would be seen by enemy aircraft —those with wavering engines that crossed on their way to bomb Liverpool, Manchester and Barrow. No bombs fell on Skipton, though it was rumoured that a cow had been hit by a bomb jettisoned by an aircraft on its return flight. Just in case 'enemy intelligence' had access to issues of the *Herald*, any information likely to be of assistance was submitted to Leeds for censoring. What would an enemy agent have made of an advert for Fog (the second growth of grass in a meadow), or the fact that Mrs Smith had won first prize in the church whist drive? Or again, that a Jam Session would be held at a youth hostel, this session being for music? (The records played would be 'from Benny Goodman to Bach and Bach again'.) Local dances were attended by Army and RAF personnel (the Royal Navy did not maintain a presence on the Leeds and Liverpool Canal). Fordson tractors with spikes on their large wheels set about ripping up the good earth for crops of grain that would grow lustily but never ripen.

The editor had a wartime job in Civil Defence, which meant that part of my work was copying manuals and drawing anti-personnel devices that might be dropped on Skipton if the enemy was truly riled. I would enter the editor's sanctum on a winter evening to find it thoroughly blacked out and thick with smoke as he incinerated cigarettes. He was economy-minded, to the extent of regularly deleting 'fish and chips' from my expenses sheet and devoting hours of time each week to cutting up government press releases so that he could turn them over and use the blank backs as 'copy' paper.

Thin and bespectacled, he liked comfort when reading proofs: he would lean back on his chair, feet on desk,

stomach serving as a desk, cigarettes, matches and ash tray
to hand. He read proofs for hours at a stretch. His trilby was
at the back of his head, his jacket open and the buttons of
his waistcoat undone. He did not like to upset any of the
readers, for that would spoil the peace and quietness of the
day. On a wall of his sanctum was a framed motto: 'Today is
the tomorrow you worried about yesterday—and all is
well.' It was. Editor John would not have it otherwise.

The advert manager had forgotten how to collect advertisements. They came to him—dozens, if not scores a day,
from grubby pieces of 'copy' to professional layouts with
metal blocks. He sat at a desk that was heaped with parcels
of all shapes and sizes. One morning, the parcel had a
curious shape and from one end of it protruded a feather.
No one had doubted, when the parcel arrived, that it
should be taken to the advert manager. Each week, he
made several journeys into the upper Dales, ostensibly to
collect advertisements. He appears to have 'done' the
books for some of the Dales farmers, who rewarded him not
with old-fashioned cash but with even older-fashioned
kind: a cock chicken or piece of pork, or even a string or two
of sausages, fragrant with herbs. He usually opened his
parcels in the quiet of another room. On this occasion I
watched him depart, heard the rustle of paper, then a lusty
roar. We rushed to his aid, to find the parcel in a corner of
the room, and near it the carcase of a large white bird, with
battalions of red mite. A note from our Grassington corre-
spondent, Sam Stables, questioned an earlier editorial decision not to use a story about an albino carrion crow that
had been seen in the dale. 'Dear Sirs,' the note began, and it
continued: 'Herewith proof that an albino carrion crow has
been seen in Wharfedale.'

A 'cub' reporter was fair game for printers. There was
Charlie Ayrton, reared at Bradley, the village in which my
grandparents had lived. Grandfather, who presided over a
village shop, had an impediment in his speech, though this
did not prevent him from serving Methodism as a local
preacher and Sunday School superintendent. Charlie loved

to tell embarrassing stories about Grandfather whenever I was passing through the 'case' room—and when there was an audience. I have already mentioned that Grandmother had a Biblical name, Selina. One November 5th, when the village lads roamed with fireworks, someone hurled a 'banger' into the shop. Whereupon my Grandfather appeared and shouted into the night, 'Top letting off them tatters! You'll tartle Telina!'

The realm of the printers, in the pre-litho age, was a grimy, smelly, noisy realm of 'hot metal', hernia-inducing equipment and oily rags. In the far recesses of the *Herald* premises, where stood an old rotary press, a throw-out from *The Yorkshire Post* in 1936, was a water tank in which the curved plates fresh from the foundry were sunk and cooled. Over the years, the water had gathered about it an unwholesome scum. Into it, periodically, a new apprentice printer was ducked to initiate him as a member of Caxton's tribe.

On the top storey were several Monotype composing machines. The operators of the keyboards punched out holes on rolls of stiffened paper. Their working lives were spent in an area of a few square yards. One man, Walter, had a quick temper and a defective little finger on his right hand; the other, whom I knew as Mr Firth, was stolid, taciturn, and crafty when it came to collecting from a table the most legible items of copy. Each day, there were a dozen arguments about a matter that could never be resolved, for every piece of copy was unique and only ten per cent worth fighting over.

Those little rolls of punched paper were sent to the casting department by gravity feed. On completing a roll, a man went to a partly opened window, undid a piece of string, slipped the string through the roll and let it slither for perhaps 30 feet until it reached the other end of the string within the casting department. Visitors commented on the system and asked what it was all about. The first time I saw the spectacle of the Descending Roll, I investigated —and came face to face with Fred, the photographer who,

years before, had begrimed the newly-decorated ceiling of
our Sunday School with his 'flash powder'. Fred had an
unenviable job, presiding over half a dozen smoking, chattering slobbering machines, from which rose scents that
would not find a place in Arcady. A blue haze obscured the
ceiling of this cell-like room. Fred's first job on arriving at
work was to remove his teeth, and show he wash not eashy
to undershtand. He was somewhat fascinated by Russia,
and whenever I met him—in his casting room or scurrying
along a passage in the building—he would say: 'What do
you think of the Rushun shituation?'

Harry Scott's formidable talents were not overstretched
by the *Herald*, especially when there were young reporters
to do his bidding. Paper rationing meant small papers, and
small papers were soon overcrowded with advertising
which did, and still does, overlap on to the front page of the
newspaper. With relatively little text to worry about, there
was no special haste, and in the afternoon we might get our
feet up on the tables and read books—until the thwack of
Reg's piece of wood on the back of the door signified
proofs. Harry Scott wrote the leading articles and, if he had
just received his rates demand, might question in the next
leader the efficiency of local government. He also provided
gossip notes for a feature called 'Craven Man's Diary', a
literary rag-bag. He carried with him a file of yellowing
cuttings taken from the Leeds newspapers during his service in the city; the topics ranged from agriculture to the
zodiac and by clever presentation could be related to
Craven. All one needed was an introduction which involved a recent meeting with 'an old Craven man', who
asked the right question or made a relevant point.

Looking back to the *Herald* days, I recall the gales of
laughter on a Friday morning when amusing errors were
revealed, a consequence of the pressure of heavy equipment on slivers of type. One week, it was the bigamy case.
The accused 'married his lawful wife' in 1941—only the first
'1' went missing. It was sheer carelessness that led to an
advertisement for Carleton Brass Band and its various

services being included in 'At Stud'. The most fascinating
tale was that of a young man who arrived at the office, and,
after telling the editor he was about to be involved in a
rather sordid court case, requested that the report should
be omitted from the *Herald*. He said he lived with his ailing
mother who would surely collapse and die if she read about
the proceedings. The editor eventually agreed that the
report would be left out of one copy of the newspaper,
which would be delivered to the young man's house. On
the following Friday, an angry man rang up to complain
that it was included, and mother was most upset. Inquiries
were made. So complex was the plan that the printers had
left the report out of every copy except one, with potentially
harmful consequences. In fact, the old lady lived on for
several years . . .

What were then called Police Courts provided us with
lots of human stories. During the time I was at the *Herald*,
nobody was murdered, mugged or raped. A scuffle between neighbouring housewives, prompted by some territorial dispute over a clothes line, held out the promise of
excitement: the case fizzled out with reconciliation. The two
ladies left the court arm-in-arm, and the defendant was
assured by her erstwhile enemy that she would pay half of
the fine. Rough-looking characters from East Lancashire
were charged with 'trespassing in pursuit of conies'. Now a
cony is a rabbit. Why not charge them with pursuing
rabbits? Years later, when I was talking to a group of
prisoners in a northern gaol, I was told by someone who
had frequently gone poaching that rabbits are vermin,
conies are game. A prosecution was under the game laws.
One character, when charged with cony-pursuing at
Broughton, a village near Skipton, said he had been on his
way to 'old Preston's place at Flasby'. Old Preston was that
day presiding on the Bench. His face went purple with
annoyance; the stiff hairs on his military-type moustache
almost twanged. He withdrew from the case, of course, but
his fellow magistrates were in no mood to be lenient.

The *Herald* was represented at important funerals. The

solemn-looking man standing at the church porch was a reporter, intent on collecting the initials of all the mourners. In the old days, the *Herald* man also collected a full list of the senders of wreaths! A funeral would have been a mournful experience but for the buoyant spirits of the Dalesfolk. I would stand on wet flagstones near the chilly little village church, looking at the names on the nearest tombstones in case any might be used for characters in the novel I always had in mind. Then along would come a crow-black party of mourners. They would dutifully tell me their names, then hang about for a few minutes, chatting and smoking. 'He didn't look so weal last time I saw him.' 'What can thou expect when somebody's getten to ninety?' 'I reckon t'Almighty must 'ev forgitten 'im.' Inside the church, there was a reverential hush and the organist played Handel's *Largo*.

We had already typed out the obituary, after consulting the Black Book, in which newspaper cuttings with biographical details were skilfully rewritten in the past tense, followed by a 'catch line', MORE TO COME, which served as a reminder to the printer making up the pages that he must look out for the appropriate funeral report and add it on. Once the 'catch line' was printed, and startled readers discovered that 'Mr Brown is survived by a wife and three daughters. MORE TO COME.'

* * *

After two years of National Service—two years before the mast, in the Navy, the mast being set in concrete—I returned to the *Herald* and a fresh set of faces. A letter arrived from Harry Scott. Would I care to visit him at Clapham and discuss plans for the future? I travelled northwards in one of the orange-sided Pennine buses that would become familiar to me in succeeding years. In those pre-bypass days, all the main road traffic passed through Clapham, the drivers nervously encountering two blind corners and a narrow, hump-backed bridge. As I disembarked near the post office, I heard the story of the Leeds lorry driver who, knocking down one of the local swans on the bridge, tossed the body over the parapet, where the regal bird lay spread-eagled across wet boulders below the waterfall. 'What were that?' asked a local man, to which the lorry driver, born and reared in a busy city, replied, 'It were nobbut a duck.'

Harry Scott welcomed me to Fellside, his home since 1935. Dorothy Scott provided a meal. In April 1939, with great courage and hardly any 'brass', he had published the first issue of a monthly magazine called *The Yorkshire Dalesman*. I remember a history lesson at school in Skipton was enlivened when the teacher, Harry Gill, held up Vol. 1, No. 1, of this periodical and commended it to us all, though at that time we were besotted with *The Hotspur* and *Dandy*. It was an effort to keep the Dales magazine alive during the war, hence Harry Scott's keenness to work part-time at the *Herald*.

Now, with the magazine almost ten years old, bearing the shorter title *The Dalesman*, and in need of further expansion, Harry asked me if I would like to join him at Clapham.

I would. And I did.

Chapter 3

In the Dales

The village of Clapham huddles against the limestone foothills of Ingleborough. It pleased me, in the early days, to explore Ingleborough, if only to discover the source of the frequently peat-stained water that emerged—I nearly made the mistake of writing 'gushed'—from the taps at Fellside. Ruskin, beholding the mountain on a windy day, had wondered how it managed to stand without rocking. A middle-aged woman, having made her first ascent, stood on the summt plateau in breezy conditions, turned to her husband and remarked, 'Wouldn't this make a good drying ground for clothes?'

It's a bleak spot—bleak enough to freeze an aspidistra, which it did in the year when the present Queen was crowned. I was approaching an almost completed Summit windbreak being built to commemorate the Coronation when I saw a plant protruding from the central well. Here, in due course, a piece of inscribed brass would be fitted. There was a note, on which the signature of Gracie Fields had been forged, claiming that this was the highest aspidistra in the land!

On one of the shoulders of Ingleborough, water trickles between the 'rush bobs' and eventually becomes a beck. The beck has scarcely time to settle down before it takes a 340-feet leap into the main chamber of a pothole, Gaping Gill, subsequently following a narrow and devious one-and-a-half mile course to emerge into daylight near the gaping mouth of a limestone cave. In those days, an estate workman, Arnold Brown, was the guide to Ingleborough

Cave, which had been discovered by the landowning Farrers in Victorian times and might now be explored for a few hundred yards with the aid of candles set on quaint, three-pronged holders. Arnold's predecessor, Harry Harrison, was something of a poet who, on taking a party to the far reaches of the show cave, offered his literary works for sale. Arnold's speciality was music of a sort, produced when he rapped the large key of the cave on some of the stalactites.

Fell Beck now made a grand progress down Clapdale, where mighty trees engaged in the ancient quest for light. The Scotts and I often walked along the old carriageway made by the Farrers and rested awhile at a shelter composed of limestone blocks and decorated by lack-lustre stumps that once had been glistening stalagmites. Where the limestone briefly gave way to slaty rocks, a famous Farrer, the rock-gardener Reginald, had planted rhododendrons and bamboos, so that the deepening little valley took on the character of a Himalayan ravine.

The lake, formed when the Farrers dammed up the valley, was in part a reservoir. Piped water, rich in tiny animal life, algae and even freshwater shrimps, flowed down one side of the village and on to some of the farms before returning to Clapham. The home of the Scotts was almost the last to be served by the local water undertaking.

The overflow from Ingleborough Lake thunders at the head of the village and takes a swift course, under many bridges, to join the Wenning. The gloomy lake was not to the liking of swans which, at the time I first knew Clapham, terrorised local people in their quest for food. Old ladies with shopping were known to sprint from the lumbering, straight-necked, hissing birds, one of whose number, as related, had perished under the wheels of a lorry.

A tale was told of a Clapham man on his visit to the market at Settle.

'Hes ta sin yon rose-coloured swan on t'lake at Clapham?' he asked a friend.

'Nay—is ta sure?'

'Aye.'

The Settle man caught the next bus to Clapham but returned disconsolately. When next he saw his Clapham friend, he said, 'I saw yon swan. It's white. Tha said it's rose-coloured.'

'So it is,' was the reply. 'There's white roses.'

Two remaining swans vanished when the beck came out in furious spate; they were next reported from a mill dam at Bentham.

On my first visit to the Scotts, a year or two before I joined *The Dalesman*, I had broken a cycle journey from a Scout camp near Kirkby Lonsdale to my home at Skipton. The cycle almost broke *me*, being unreliable and with a pedal that struck the frame at every revolution. One of my fellow Scouts had packed me some sandwiches. He used most of a loaf, cut the slices nearly an inch thick—and by no means straight—and used some tinned luncheon meat as filling. I slipped the packet under my shirt as I mounted the bike. By the time I reached Clapham, the sandwiches were bonded into one piece of a doughy substance that was first-cousin to a bread poultice. I dismounted by the Brokken Bridge and wheeled the bike across. A large piece of bread slithered to the ground. I hastily tossed it over the parapet. There was a joyful quacking sound. A second piece became food for local sparrows. By the time I reached the gate leading to the door of Fellside, the bread poultice was in rapid disintegration. One lump descended on the blue-grey flags of the garden path, another in the hall and the last on the living room carpet.

Another time, Harry Scott had taken delivery of an issue of *The Dalesman*. Piles of copies were stacked in the hall and adjacent rooms. Mrs Scott, with artistic skill, had disguised some of the heaps as small tables, with attractively-embroidered clothes to cover them and bowls of flowers to claim the attention. Visitors were always welcome, for magazine-packing had become a cottage industry. We sat for hours, yarning, drinking coffee, slipping magazines into the brown 9"×6" envelopes, on which names and addresses were typed by hand in a tedious operation involving rolls of labels.

Rarely can a country magazine have been produced in such an unspoilt rural setting. The day was punctuated by bleating as flocks of sheep were driven backwards and forwards, attended by yapping dogs. In spring and summer, curlews glided overhead, uttering their heart-stirring trills.

Harry Scott's editorials were conversational in manner, as though he was writing a chatty note to old friends. Sitting at his desk, his pipe aglow and blue-grey smoke rising like incense, he wrote quickly, with pencil, using newsprint, leaving the customary space between lines for subbing.

It has been a mark of the pleasant friendly bond which has always existed between this magazine and its readers that almost from our first appearance our title was shortened in conversation, in letters and over bookstall counters to 'The Dalesman' (he noted). Such a curtailment of our title has continually encouraged us, for when Thomas becomes Tom and when Elizabeth is shortened to Betty, it is conclusive that they are adopted as one of the household, or at least an intimate friend of the family. Such, we believe, has been our privilege . . .

Of a recently acquired arts magazine, *Northern Review*, he wrote: 'It is proposed to remodel this as a literary and artistic miscellany for the North of England, and the first number will be published early in May.' The price was announced as 2s. Not many issues were published. It was not the right time for such an enterprise. Readers were few in number and advertisements scarce.

* * *

On my first day, Harry yarned about the magazine he had begun ten years before. He recalled spending a weekend at

Burford, in Oxfordshire, with his older namesake, Robert-son Scott, who had founded *The Countryman* and main-tained it with considerable authority. Harry was offered a job—and declined it. He acknowledged that Robertson Scott was a remarkable editor, but he was also 'a bit of an autocrat'. Also, it would have meant that he and his family would be called upon to live in the 'softer South . . . it just wasn't my countryside!'

The original print order for *The Yorkshire Dalesman* was 3,000 copies; the printing bill came to £25. The magazine had achieved a monthly circulation of 4,000 when wartime paper control was introduced. Having been published for only six months, and with the paper allocation based on the previous 12 months' consumption, supplies were cut in half. Yet by reducing the weight and quality of paper used, Harry Scott maintained the 4,000 circulation through the war years. Fascinating tales were told of how copies turned up all over the world, including a Shanghai hotel, in a Cassino dug-out and in the middle of Africa. When a copy was lost because of enemy action, a letter would be received asking for a replacement. If spare copies existed, they were despatched. Subscribers added small bonus amounts to their subscriptions or sent gifts 'to help you tide over difficult times'.

With an unsatisfied demand, the magazine's circulation leapt up as soon as paper was freely available. By 1946, it had risen to 10,000. At the time I joined, it was almost 20,000 (and would put on another 10,000 over the next decade).

Clapham, at that time, had scarcely changed its appear-ance for 30 years, though the days had gone when local people touched their forelocks or curtsyed to the folk from the big house. Indeed, the Farrers had left Inglebor-ough Hall, and when I first knew the estate Matthew Rowland Farrer occupied a smaller house than the agent, Claude Barton, whose residence was Hall Garth. It was Charlie Leach, of the *Telegraph and Argus*, who told me of his only visit to the latter. He had been attending a pothole incident on the flanks of Ingleborough and was anxious to telephone the story to his paper in Bradford. He was directed to Hall Garth. Here, a woman welcomed him, allowed him to telephone and then took him into a room where a meal was laid out. The hungry journalist almost 'cleared the deck'. In conversation, the woman said, 'We all like *The Yorkshire Post* in Clapham.' The embarrassed Charlie fled before Nemesis arrived in the shape of the agent or the reporter from the rival newspaper.

My first lodgings were with Hetty Turner, who lived just below the school. It was an estate house, slate-cold and reeking of paraffin, which was used for lighting, heating and cooking. Hetty gave me a Yorkshire welcome, which meant enough food to 'hod your back up', a cheerful fireside and a snug bed. I was sent to sleep by the calls of local tawny owls—the hoots of the males and sharp 'kewicks' of the females. I awoke to more curlew calls or the sound of cattle being driven to the shippon for milking; hand-milking in most cases, the milk spurting in short, sharp bursts against the sides of the pails.

The Sub-Postmaster was an excellent weather forecaster, though he had an urban background. 'It's going to rain,' he said. And it did. I asked him how he knew, and he remarked, 'A sheet of new stamps was curling.' Ben Hudson, however, an old farmer who I felt sure would be an even better forecaster, did not immediately answer when I asked him what the Weather Clerk had in mind. We were standing under cover of a barn porch as the rain 'siled' down. Ben looked at the sky, where dark clouds were fast-moving. He looked at the beck—for what reason I could not understand. Then he looked at his feet. Perhaps they ached when bad weather was in prospect. Eventually, he looked at me and said, 'It could do owt.' One of his farming pals, a rather narrow-minded Chapelgoer, refused to say Hello because 'it's "O Hell" the wrong way round.'

Clapham 40 years ago was like a film-set, waiting for something to happen. The church tower was conspicuously old; the rest of the building had been re-erected last

century to the greater glory of God and the folk at the Big
House. The Vicarage had been built at a time when all
self-respecting vicars kept a large staff of servants. I used to
'camp' Canon Simpson and hear him yarn about Old
Oireland in a gentle Irish voice. Once he drove me in his car
to a lecture appointment in a nearby village. He had an
individualistic style, rarely staying on his own side of the
road and needing his handbrake to correct his high speed
on corners. He brought his little car to a halt in the centre of
the road when he had switched off the lights by mistake.
'We'll wait until this lorry passes. Then I'll look for the
switch,' he said, with no trace of anxiety.

Each morning, shortly before nine, I walked up the
village. There was time for a chat with Sam West, the
postman, whose great moment came each November
when, clad in his Sunday best, and with a couple of rows
of medals, he led a small procession of fellow British
Legioners to the war memorial to lay a wreath. Grannie
Cross would be working in her cottage garden—both she
and the garden were tiny. It was said that whenever she
acquired a new plant she had to ponder hard and long on
which of the existing plants should be removed to make
way for it. Grannie had come to the village as servant girl at
the Vicarage; she stayed on, married, bore a large family
and became a most respected member of the community,
law-abiding in all things but plant collections. On outings,
she invariably carried an umbrella, whatever the weather.
Into it went cuttings hastily taken from any plants that took
her fancy and which would scarcely feel the loss of the tip of
one of their many points of growth.

To walk anywhere in the parish of Clapham could be
hazardous. I was chased by a bull at Keasden, by geese on
Newby Green and 'wild' horses that roamed on and around
Newby Moor. They were young animals which had been
turned out to graze an unfenced tract of ground that had
herbage in abundance and on which local farmers had
grazing rights. Now and again the horses stampeded,
possibly through sheer high spirits. As I walked up the road

from the railway station and heard the thunder of hooves, I
would slip over the nearest wall to avoid the drove of
playful animals careering by. They were 'culled' by local
traffic over a period of years. The van of the Austwick
butcher claimed one, and another fell victim to a Pennine
bus, the driver of which could hardly be expected to see a
black horse standing broadside on the road on a wild night:
the bus's headlamps produced only a weak yellow beam.
When three horses remained on the Moor, the owners
quietly took them back home.

Looking over the downstream parapet of the main
bridge, and seeing water creaming over rocks, to bubble
and swirl in a deep pool, I was reminded of what I had been
told of Clapham during the period of food rationing. It was
a time when butcher and grocer needed coupons for essential supplies and when inspectors tracked down illegal pigs
with the fervour once shown over illicit whisky stills. It
seems that a northward-bound van, full of tinned food, left
the road near the New Inn and plunged into the beck,
spilling much of its cargo. The God-fearing, previously
law-abiding villagers turned into a gang of wreckers, removing as many tins as they could manage and not forgetting to deliver some to the home of the policeman (who was
then ill in bed). Months later, the more adventurous young
folk went 'fishing' for tins in the deeper part of the pool.

While crossing t'Brokken Bridge—a single-span structure—I would stop and watch a dipper 'bobbing' on one of
the water-smoothed boulders. Sometimes, when the beck
was low, I could see the plump, dark brown bird with its
white bib walking under water, its head down, facing the
current, which flowed over its inclined back and kept it
against the bed of the stream where its food was found.
Once, a kingfisher darted like a fragment of rainbow
through a patch of sunlight. And always, in spring and
summer, there were curlews, climbing in the warm air with
powerful wingbeats, pausing, then gliding slowly earth-
wards, filling the sky with their fluty trills.

The Dalesman office was what would normally have been

the lounge of Fellside (or t'parlour, to anyone reared in the
Dales). The central space was occupied by a huge wooden
desk, forming a good working surface and with lots of
cupboards at the sides. I was never quite sure if the walls
were papered or not because they were lagged with
books—thousands of books.

Harry Scott had contrived to move into this nerve centre
of his publishing operation two of the common-or-garden
green metal, four-drawer filing cabinets. On top of one was
a wooden tray, with cards relating to *Dalesman* postal
subscribers. There were not many of them. He reckoned
that in those days anyone with a telephone must be
affluent, so the first hour of the day was spent writing
names and addresses from a telephone directory onto those
ubiquitous 9"×6" brown envelopes.

Sometimes, the work was varied, and we copied onto
envelopes the names and addresses of a private organisation, culled from the back of the annual report. Surplus
copies of *The Dalesman* were thus spread about the face of
Britain. One month, dog-lovers would be bombarded; the
next, it would be the turn of former pupils of a well-known
independent school; then it was back to the telephone
directory. A torrent of copies went out, a trickle of new
subscribers came back, but it was on this pioneering type
of mail-shot that the circulation of the magazine rose
steadily, from about 20,000 to 40,000 and ultimately to over
70,000.

Jobs came in bewildering variety—an article to write,
some letters to file, an advertising scheme to initiate,
adverts to collect, sometimes using that curious old bike
which had first brought me to Clapham. Cups of coffee or
tea appeared, brought by Dorothy Scott or by Doreen
Shaw, who worked for the Scotts. Elsie Dickinson attended
to the subscriptions and some of the accounts, working
from the upper room at Knowles's grocer's shop in
Bentham. I used to meet a morning bus with a bundle of
forms for Elsie. Also catching the bus would be Mrs Vant,
with a pet mallard in her shopping basket.

The Scotts were Quakers. Harry Scott was rarely excited or annoyed. His favourite word was 'amiable' and it seemed to reflect his character. I began to think of him as the last of the Edwardian publishers. He worked in the traditional way, with soft pencil on soft 'copy' paper. There was an old-time charm about his writing. When the pencil was not skimming the paper, he was sucking his pipe, as he impulsively commissioned a book. At that time, I was smoking a considerable number of cigarettes a day, so the atmosphere could be as muggy as that around a Bradford mill with a rush-order for cloth.

He spent most of his working life in carpet slippers, to the extent of forgetting to change his footwear for one of his periodic jaunts to Leeds for a look-round and a haircut: he found himself in City Square with slippers on his feet. Buying a new pair of shoes led to some restraint on the magazine, for he was living hand-to-mouth at that time, his operations financed by the 10s 6d postal orders as they arrived from subscribers. It was amusing to see him put some in his wallet when he was about to set off on one of his occasional excursions.

When he was not working, he was reading. He read everything that was to hand—a book, magazine, leaflet or even a paper from one of the heaps of old *Yorkshire Posts* that were always within reach. The fact that they were a quarter of a century out of date delighted him.

Mrs Scott was small and dark. Wiry and active, she was rarely still, hopping on and off buses on market day, spending sunny hours in the garden, developing proficiency as a water-colourist and helping needy old ladies in the village. She ran Fellside and helped with the magazine. The family was completed by two children, Margaret and Martin; they were away at school for most of the time during my early years at Clapham.

Visitors were welcome. Professor Joad, of BBC radio fame, came down off Ingleborough dripping wet and had a hot bath while his clothes were dried before the fire. On the wireless, Joad presaged each point he made with: 'It all depends what you mean by . . .' The Scotts waited in vain for him to use it in everyday speech.

To have a bath was an achievement in an area where the arterial water-pipe was old and inclined to burst and when pressure was usually low. Water merely trickled out of our taps twice a day, when the farmers were cooling milk with a fluted appliance that relied on a flow of cold water.

When my stay with Hetty Turner ended—it was for but a few months—I was found accommodation at nearby Austwick, in the home of a quite remarkable lady, Maude Bacon—henceforth to be known as Mrs B.

Chapter 4

East of Clapham

You could not find two adjacent villages more different from each other than Clapham and Austwick. An ancient rivalry existed, with shouts of 'Clapham carls' or 'Austwick clouts' whenever a man from one village was seen in the other. Clapham, of estate origin, was predominantly Victorian, being tucked up snugly in the mouth of Clapdale, whereas I found that Austwick folk had a sturdy independence. The village itself received protection from Norber, the north hill, but otherwise has an open situation.

When the day's work was over, I would follow the footpath through the fields to Austwick, where Mrs B awaited me with the day's gossip and a hot meal. At Clapham, the footpath passed between Ben Hudson's farmyard and Jack Winton's garden. I sometimes found them engaged in heated talk. Ben's hens were fond of crossing the path into the mini-jungle of Jack's well-kept plot, where there was much greenery to peck and a wealth of insect life unknown in the arid farmyard. Jack frequently told Ben about the trespass, but Ben could 'do nowt about it'.

One day, Jack's voice had lost its rasping sound—and Ben looked concerned. I heard later that the gardener had mentioned to the farmer that he was about to spray his garden with poison; he didn't want the hens to be affected. Their nomadic life ended. Ben shifted them to another part of his farm.

The footpath unfolded with many a pleasant vista. A cock wheatear played hide and seek with me, dodging behind a stretch of wall. Eventually Austwick lay before me, a village built of native stone and substantial roof flags; it seemed to be tethered to the hills by a network of walls. There was usually time for a chat with Johnny Hargreaves, who would be out 'kenning' his livestock. Two brothers, collectively known as Jimmy-Johnny, farmed on the low ground but had some hillside pastures to give their prize cattle a change of grazing.

Johnny's means of transport was a pony with a tub-like trap. As he reined in the pony on the skyline, to look hard and long at his 'bee-asts', I thought of him as some latter-day Caesar, surveying his troops.

'Grand day?'

'Aye.'

Or perhaps it was early spring, starvation time for animals, with the conditions cold and wet.

'What's gone wrong with the weather?'

'Nay,' replied Johnny, pausing in the counting of sheep, 'this'll mak t'owd yows bleat for a bit o' fodder.' (Translation: 'In this cold weather, the sheep will be feeling hungry.')

After chatting with Johnny, I descended to a stile. Beyond lay the home of Mrs B. It was not a typical Pennine house, the sort that looked venerable and grey, with mullioned windows and a seventeenth century date above the door. Mrs B owned a semi-detached house such as was built by the thousand in pre-war England. The name beside the door, Rothbury, proclaimed her origins in the North-East. She and her family had arrived in Austwick from Headingley in Leeds. The family had dispersed. She remained, with her garden, her bees, her membership of the Parochial Church Council and the Women's Institute—'jam and Jerusalem'—plus croquet.

Mrs B moved briskly, had a firm handclasp, was a good cook and, believing that the Devil has work for idle hands, contrived to remain busy from before dawn until after dusk. When she periodically sat down, it was to test her wits against the compiler of *The Yorkshire Post* crossword. Then the spectacles that usually dangled before her on a

length of band were perched on her nose. In between
finding answers to clues, her fingers crackled with surplus
nervous energy.

She did her best to stop the headlong rush into Modern-
ism, opposing street lighting, new forms of worship at the
church and the strange new morality under which good
and evil were no longer distinct. She always did things in
style. During a visit to a brother in America, she had not
been able to resist buying some American novelties, including a card shuffler, which henceforth occupied prime space
on the card table.

To be invited to 'Elevenses' was to experience an event
conducted in Edwardian splendour—it was not just a
matter of making half a dozen cups of instant coffee. As
practised by Mrs B, 'Elevenses' was a grand occasion, more
'Headingley' than 'Dales', and absolutely nothing to do
with assuaging thirst or combating hunger-knock.

The sitting room, like the British Empire, had about it a
faded glory. Talk tended to range over serious matters, for
wisecracks would have been inappropriate against a background of antique furniture and wallpaper that was heavily
patterned, with a vaguely floral theme. The visitors stirred
and sipped and went through the usual delaying tactics
with regard to the food, anxious not to be thought glut-
tonous. I usually stared at some of the wooden objects
adorning the room—items which an uncle had fashioned
during the fretwork craze, and pieces of carved woodwork
collected during holidays in Switzerland. Woe betide anyone who surreptitiously lifted a piece of carved wood, for it
was ten to one there was a primed musical box lurking
underneath.

The cake-stand was folded up when not in use. On active
service, it needed the weight of a few cakes to give it
stability. The sandwiches were refined—thin and wedge-
shaped—being 'three to the gobful', as one guest had
indiscreetly remarked. The scones were diminutive and
crumbly: a generous application of butter was needed
to keep the pieces together. The principal cake had

layers of sponge encompassing home-made raspberry jam.

Guests came not just for 'Elevenses': they were there for 'Twelveses' as well. The company consisted mainly of spinsters and widows, who wore outfits with a modicum of jewellery. One spinster was so small and thin I entertained the fantastic thought that when she had a cup of tea she would look like a thermometer. A heavily-built woman, wearing tweeds and men's-type shoes, was noted for her stories of foreign travel, and could also be relied upon to enliven a discussion about 'modern' education by her general denunciation of anything that had happened since 1926. A third guest wore a two-piece and one of those repulsive fox furs. The head of the fox, with its beady eyes, had its mouth attached to the base of the 'brush' to keep this bizarre decoration in position.

Summertime was devoted by Mrs B to mowing her lawn, collecting and preserving raspberries, manipulating three beehives, catering for the welfare of free-range hens, attending to housework, making a hot meal each evening and keeping alert in case Hilda, her neighbour, shouted 'Pig', which was not a term of abuse but alerted Mrs B to the fact that her porker had once again broken out of the pen and was about to plough up the croquet lawn with its snout, questing for worms.

The shout came during my very first meal at Austwick. The food was hastily returned to the oven to keep warm. We dashed down the garden to find that the pig, having brushed against one of the supports of the hen hut—which now tilted—was indeed on the lawn. We coaxed it back into the pen, added a few more yards of wire to the tangled mess and returned to the meal.

The lawn was tended with an almost religous fervour, for upon the mowing depended the quality of the evening play. One dressed for croquet! With pig, hens and bees remaining from the wartime impulse to augment the weekly food ration, little space remained on Mrs B's third of an acre for a conventional lawn: its shape was irregular, having accommodated such afterthoughts as extra fruit trees and a row of bee hives.

Croquet was played between the greenhouse and a vegetable patch. Mrs B had made her garden from a corner of a field—Harry Holden had walled it off for her—and a lawn that looked flat was far from being so. The croquet-player who knew about the local topography could do wonderful things with one of the large wooden balls.

After tea, neighbours who did not wish to play croquet tended to move about their houses on all-fours, so that they would not be seen above the level of the window ledges. Anyone who stirred would be invited to join in games that began with the sun high in the sky and ended in the moonlight, with somone producing a match to check on the colour of a ball that was just a dark orb in the gloaming.

If the bees were lively, the game was inclined to be jerky, all but Mrs B rushing past the hives, conscious that for a few yards the line between two croquet hoops was within easy stinging distance of the main flightlines of the bees. Once or twice in the summer, a hive seemed to boil over as bees swarmed, but help was at hand in the form of John, the local joiner and undertaker. I would don a netted hat and gloves and watch with drooping lower jaw as the two, gentle-mannered, took a straw skep, held it under the place on the apple tree where a brown, syrupy mass of bees lay, and coaxed the bees into the skep. They played the timeless game of follow-my-leader, in this case the queen. I usually kept my distance, though Mrs B assured me the bees would not sting. 'They're sated with honey.'

I did move closer in the late evening. It was fascinating to see the swarm transferred to an empty hive—to watch the regal progress of the queen up a running board and to see with what devotion the rest of the community attended her. Mrs B was concerned when part of this dark brown army, many of them potential stingers, followed a route that lay over her bare leg or across feet that were encased in floppy sandals. She did not want any of the bees to be injured. 'Don't go there, lovey,' she crooned, and carefully removed a bee from the gap between two of her toes.

I was present when the Austwick Tigers went on the warpath. The name was given to some vicious bees owned by Norman Burniston and kept in the walled garden at the back of the house where he lived with his mother. John and Mrs B were assisting him to do work on a hive when the denizens suddenly appeared as a far from placid swarm. With a reckless disregard for their own well-being, they fastened themselves on Norman's face and zoomed angrily around the netting which protected ours.

The summer evening faded into greys and blues. We stood in the garden, at a level with the bedroom window, through which we could see the hapless Norman swathed in an eiderdown and uttering (muffled) curses against bees. We heard the sound of the front door being opened, and realised it was his elderly mother returning home after a day spent with friends. A light was switched on. Bees that had found cosy corners with the onset of dusk were now coaxed into the open by this artificial sun and buzzed around it, attended by shrieks from Norman's mother. A fortnight later, the Austwick Tigers had been sold.

*   *   *

Austwick was characterful then. I define a character as an individual, someone who makes up his or her mind about things rather than taking opinions second-hand. It helps if the character is somewhat eccentric, as was Mr Coates, the old man who never went to bed. He slept in a chair before the fire in his tiny cottage, surrounded by bags of cinders. Either he was unsure what to do with them or he could not bear to part with them.

David Jack (Pritchard) was another whose doings caused the saner members of the community to shake their heads sadly. He spent much of his life sitting before the fire. On the hearth was a large basin, into which he would pour a quarter-pound packet of tea, periodically adding water when he was thirsty. When the tea had lost its strength he simply tossed the old leaves on the fire and poured another packet of tea into the basin. What could be simpler?

With the Austwick Field Club, I explored the district—up onto the lunar-like landscape of Norber, where we heard the soulful whistle of the golden plover and saw a gold-and-black bird standing sentinel on the skyline. Ravens nested on the crags of Moughton. Each spring, the children of the village went forth to collect the eggs, but were never successful. *En route*, one of their number would fall and graze a leg, resulting in the expedition being called off. I loved to approach the nest in misty or windy weather, when I hoped to see a sitting bird. A hoarse croaking drew attention to the ravens in flight. A bird playfully flicked over onto its back and flew upside down for a spell. We had an outing 'down the beck for birds', which included sandpiper and the oystercatcher—another piper, with a pied plumage.

The best-known naturalist, Chris Cheetham, became a special friend. The first time I went botanising with him, we tramped towards the wooded slopes of Oxenber. I ranged over a field, looking for splashes of red, yellow or blue. He knelt on the ground and pointed out a dozen different plants in an area the size of my handkerchief. He was forever inviting me to taste the leaves he plucked from various plants, and I recall in particular the cucumber flavour of salad burnet. A species of daddy-long-legs was named after him, *Tipula cheethami*, and he was an authority on mosses and lichens. He had taken the first opportunity to leave employment in the West Riding textile industry. He never shaved, nor did he wear long trousers. He had joined the Cyclists' Touring Club in 1890, shortly after it was formed, and when he was over 70 and his mother over 90 he used to take her out—on a tandem. When I last saw him alive, we climbed Oxenber. Chris had just come out of hospital, having had a metal hinge put in his hip, so we chose a route that was kindest to his hip. He bemoaned the stiffness and said it was a pity that the surgeon who performed the operation had not left a hole through which he could oil the hinge!

If there is a recognisable Heaven, then Chris will be in the choir. He loved singing hymns and was a member of the church choir. For good measure, he attended any convenient Methodist services. I found myself sharing in a rugged form of Methodism. Many of the local preachers were farmers or farm men, who had a no-holds-barred attitude towards religion. There were two classifications —'saved' and 'sinner'—and there was an emotional blackmail on the 'sinner' until he or she was shamed into 'coming down to the front of the Chapel' at some mission, there to 'accept Christ'.

Mrs B felt somewhat uneasy with Methodists and she regularly attended the parish church. As for me, a townie until recently, I was often amazed at the religious excesses —the loud 'Hallelujahs' and 'Amens' to be heard as a local preacher prayed fervently (and somewhat repetitively); the frequent use of dialect (hadn't Christ spoken dialect?); the attempts at humour and the earthy illustrations. A preacher who told what he considered to be amusing tales once earned a gale of laughter when he illustrated the power of prayer according to his experiences on his last visit to a hillside chapel. He had been cycling into a strong headwind, and he prayed that God might change its direction. 'God answered my prayer,' he said, adding, 'It sarved me reight for thinkin' about missen. There were a head-wind when I cycled home!'

Austwick Chapel was not the most evangelical in the district. When I first knew it, one could be assured of a large congregation and lusty singing, accompanied by music on an organ which was hand-pumped. A wooden handle protruded from the side, and Mr Batty, who operated it, kept his eye on a lead pellet at the end of a string, his guide as to how much air remained in the bellows. At the extremes were pencil marks—empty and full. A wit had written above 'full' the word 'bust'.

When Mrs Fawcett was playing the organ, she liked to

spread her fingers and press hard on the keys when one of
the Wesley hymns was being performed. The luckless
organ-blower had to work furiously to maintain the air
pressure. A story was told of the time the organ stopped
during the singing of 'Fight the Good Fight'. The organ-
blower was heard to lament, 'T' fight's ower—cord's
brokken.'

The great days of Chapel-going were in the past, but here
and there one might come across a chapel with every seat
filled and virtually the whole district present, from the
latest baby in a carry-cot to the oldest grandfather.
Strangers, unaccustomed to rural fervour, were unprepared for the furious hymn-singing. The exhalation of air
almost pinned the preacher against the back wall of the
chapel. Prayers were uttered amid a chorus of 'Amens'.
Sermons were just beginning to warm the congregation up
after 20 minutes.

I should have realised, when visiting this chapel, that the
average dalesman does not have a fanciful streak: realism is
the quality one best remembers. I was a little fanciful in my
children's address—after all, it was for young people—and
I was unprepared when an old chap rose to his feet and
shouted, 'We want none o' thee fairy tales here!' He did
apologise afterwards. He came selfconsciously towards me
and said, gruffly, 'Sorry I'd to speak during t'service.' And I
simply replied, 'So am I.'

Chapter 5

A Spirited People

My first article for *The Dalesman* was headed 'Old Mick—the bull walloper'. It dealt with Michael Raynard, a Settle character renowned not just for his ability to drive cattle but also because he was said to drink 12 pints to 12 strokes of the clock, a feat made possible because he had no Adam's apple and therefore poured the stuff down his throat like liquid down a drain. It was a strange start to a career in monthly journalism, especially for a quiet lad who was also a Methodist. My first claim for expenses at *The Dalesman* included the item: 'Five pints of ale . . .'

The emblem of old Mick's cattle droving days was a hazel switch, with its strong powers of persuasion in the right hands. To chat with him was to become aware of the half-savage life of the itinerant countryman who has no settled life. He drifted down to Settle from Carlisle. The local people were good to him, so he stayed.

He told of travelling from Skipton to Pateley Bridge late one evening when he entered an old quarry and discovered a cabin, the door of which had been blown open by the wind. He decided on sleep and settled down on some bracken. About the middle of the night, he was aware of 'something' coming into the hut. 'I just said "shoo" to it, but it started sniffing over me. I jumped up, and thought the Devil had come for me, but it was only an old donkey. I had taken its bed.'

I travelled about the Dales by bus, train or Shanks' pony. In 1950, a short walk took me over the hill from Rawlinshaw to Feizor, yet I beheld this hidden hamlet with all the excitement of someone who had found himself in the headwaters of the Amazon. Half a dozen houses and farms brooded quietly in a steel-grey mist. There were no signs of modernity, not even telephone posts at the roadside.

Frederic Riley, author and bookseller, had a cottage there. He told me of the sage, John Wilman, who on nights when clouds swept over the fells and hid the moon, would stare upwards and remark that 't'village lantern's gone out.' And so it was at the time of my visit. When the moon was obscured, the only public lighting was not in operation. Oil lamps flickered at the farms and storm lanterns in the outhouses. The average household was using between six and eight gallons of paraffin a month.

I crossed the watershed and descended to Wensleydale. Now I began to meet some rare old characters—men such as George Metcalfe, of Appersett. He was seated by the bridge, clay pipe in mouth, old cap high on the back of his head and well down over his eyes, and high cheeks bristling with grey hairs that eventually merged with a bushy moustache. He told me he had never seen the sea. A pause. 'I isn't anxious to see t'sea. It's only watter.'

We chatted about the drystone walls that are among the Seven Wonders of the Dales. George had erected many a rood of wall—for 3s a rood, which in Yorkshire was counted as seven yards. Visitors marvel at what one American called 'those cute stone fences'. Each stretch of wall is really two walls in one, bound together with 'throughs', tapering with height, the gap between the two sides filled with rubble, and with topstones to turn the weather and protect the main part of the wall. George told me that the stones he used came from old walls, from river beds and from 'grey beds' (limestone outcrops). He had been taught the skills by his father who once, when building a wall over a hilltop, had to barrow his materials 30 or 40 yards uphill. 'I can tak thee to walls I med 60 year sin—an' there's still plenty o' life in 'em.'

To reach Littondale, a tributary valley of the Wharfe, I travelled by bus—being the only passenger as it neared the head of the dale. I walked back as far as Kilnsey, where a Dales farmer driving a lorry stopped to pick me up. He said generously, 'Tha can get in t'cab, on t'back or on t'running board.' The cab contained the farmer, two friends and a couple of dogs, the back was half-full of steaming manure; so I stood on the running board and was borne quickly, if not in style, to Grassington.

In Littondale, almost 40 years ago, the roadman was a familiar figure. Harry Moule told me that he was returning home to Halton Gill at 5 p.m. one autumn evening when he heard a cackling of hens and saw a fox watching them. The fox was so close to the wall, Harry quietly removed a capstone from the wall and dropped it on the animal.

The old Dales life was still a vivid memory. John Campbell, of Halton Gill, told me of the farmer living at remote Cosh who each year mowed 18 acres with a scythe. Haytimers at Skipton had been demanding £40 for a month's work. 'They got about £4 when I was a lad . . . My father got £1 a week—and browt up 11 of us. The cost of living was modest, with butter costing 9d a pound.'

I met the Ingilbys at Nether Hesleden and heard of the salving days, when a mixture of butter and Stockholm tar, 'wi' a drop o' milk to take the sting out of it', was applied to the skin of a sheep, the wool having been parted or 'shedded'. Salved sheep were supposed to winter better than untouched animals. William Ingilby said, 'I've salved thousands of sheep . . . Salve made your hands black. My eldest brother was married at salving time. His hands were jet black for the ceremony.'

I was impressed by the spirit of the dalesfolk. It was pleasant to enter a smithy on a chilly day, to see the active forge, with the glow of the embers merging the room into a cosy pattern of orange-red light and shadow. The Wilsons of Settle were musical blacksmiths, for after a working day they played for dances up and down the Dales. Harry Wilson had first become interested in playing at dances when he attended one at Stainforth and found his feet tapping to the music provided by Kit Graham's Band. They had taken their piano with them on a flat cart! They charged 15s and entertained until 2 a.m. Harry had played at a genuine barn dance; a cart cover was placed across the doors to cheat the wind.

At Hawes, John Oswald Dinsdale, aged 74, was completing a long career at the smithy. He recalled for me the days of 'blood for money'. He was knocked about by the 'stags', the unbroken ponies, fresh from the breeding grounds on the fells, which were sold at the autumnal horse fair. Many ponies were bought by the horse-and-cart dealers of the northern towns. When breaking in a lively pony, some dalesmen filled an old pair of trousers with straw and strapped them to the back of the animal, which soon discovered what it would be like to carry a man.

A blacksmith had to be something of a vet. He docked horse tails and knocked out 'wolf' teeth, which formed in front of grinders. The 'wolves' were extracted by hammer and chisel. Before the coming of the railways and motor transport, Mr Dinsdale's father had made foot plates for cows. A striking tribute to the skill and versatility of the bygone craftsmen of the Dales was when father and grandfather made a 'penny-farthing' bicycle from the design of one that had been briefly left outside the smithy. It was done without blueprints or, as the Dales craftsman might have said, 'by t'rack o' t'eye'.

At Kilnsey, I met three sisters and heard about the women's role in Dales life, especially in the remote areas, abutting the wilderness. Katherine, Sarah and Annie were born into the Ingilby family of Littondale. At the turn of the century, Katherine was delivering the mail at some of the dalehead farms. Twice a week, she rode her pony to Halton Gill, thence along the wild road 'back o' Penyghent'. She also visited Cosh farmstead. Her wage was 4s a week.

Sarah mentioned the days when oatcake was a staple food in the Dales; when made, she hung it on a rack, where the coarse strips resembled wash-leathers as they dried in the heat of the kitchen fire. Any surplus milk was made into butter: on some days she would help to produce between 60 lb and 80 lb. It was sold at 9d a pound. Much later, when milk was leaving the farms as milk, in shiny kits, the collecting lorry could not reach Upper Wharfedale, the road having been blocked by snow; milk that would normally have been thrown away was made into butter.

The image in my mind when I wrote about the Dales was the windswept upland, with outcropping rock, walls, a few thorn trees, sheep and the indomitable Dales farmer—not forgetting his dog. Gilbert Brown, of Malham, was a shepherd in his younger days and then worked on 'the lonely old roads of Malham Moor'. Prior to the motor age, dalesfolk made their own entertainment in Malham. Gilbert Brown told me there were only two dances a year, 'but we made a good job of them!' My first association with Malham was as a Methodist local preacher, baht (without) car, who travelled by Pennine bus to Airton, took the morning service, walked up to Cousin Janet's at Calton for lunch (complete with home-made ice cream) and then took the riverside route to Malham, where worshippers awaited at the Chapel and a splendid tea followed at a house in the village. I would walk to the head of Malham Cove, where the weathered limestone outcrops looked like segments of a giant brain. Then it was back for the evening service—and a sprint to the bus stop to catch the last bus of the day back to Skipton.

Gilbert Brown was among the worshippers at Malham. He had a fund of good stories. He told me of a man who put a half sovereign into the collection plate instead of a sixpence and afterwards approached the steward and mentioned his plight.

'If thou taks that 'alf sovereign back, tha'll be damned,' the steward said.

'Aye,' was the doleful response, 'and if Ah doan't tak it back Ah'll be beggered!'

There were many such tales. My favourite was of the lady who insisted on taking a family Bible to Chapel and rested it on her knees during the sermon. One summer afternoon, as the preacher droned on, she fell asleep and the Bible fell to the ground with a thwack. She awoke with a start and demanded of her husband, 'What's ta brokken now?'

I walked for miles through Wharfedale when the number of vehicles that passed might be reckoned at half a dozen an hour. A farm man would pass on a pedal bike, a can of milk strapped to his back. The roadman would be hard at work with a shovel, familiar with every quirk of the local highway and its drainage system. He, too, would have a bike, with an old mackintosh thrown over the handlebars and an ex-Army pack containing cold tea and sandwiches hanging from a handlebar. I found special pleasure at Hubberholme, with its ancient church so close to the brawling Wharfe that after a serious flood the waters abated to reveal fish between the pews—pews which, incidentally, have the mouse carving of Thompson, the Kilburn craftsman. On my first visits, Harry Isherwood was the vicar. He was fond of telling me of the time when Colin Wills, a broadcaster, had chatted with him upon the bridge at Hubberholme. When the vicar mentioned that the turbulent Wharfe had upset the fabric of the church, the broadcaster held the microphone so that listeners might hear the sound of the water. Thousands of miles away, in Hong Kong, a soldier was listening to the broadcast. He was a Falshaw, an Upper Wharfedale man. He had the heart-warming experience of hearing the river of his native dale.

Fred Falshaw, the postman, was a never failing source of entertaining stories. Before a bridge was built across the river near New House Farm, Fred used to ford the Wharfe with the letters. At low water, this was easy. He simply walked from one rounded stone to another. In a spate, he could not undertake the crossing. Once, as he stood by the swollen river, the farmer arrived. Fred tied a postcard to a stone and threw it across the water. The stone landed at the farmer's feet; the postcard became detached and was blown into the water, to be swept away. The farmer watched its departure. 'Nivver mind abut it now,' he said. 'What wer on't?'

The postbox at Beckermonds was once covered with

snow for six weeks. Fortunately, it had just been cleared before the blizzard.

In the days before the Dales roads heard the regular whine and whoosh of speeding traffic, drovers with cattle and sheep were commonplace and men like Kit Wiseman, of Kettlewell, were the local carriers. With a horse called Boxer that stood 17 hands high, Kit used carts made locally by John Raw, the wooden wheels being hooped with iron by the local blacksmith, Benjamin Ward.

Kit, when an old man, told me that he often made an early morning call on Benjamin when the weather 'turned nasty' and the roads were slippery, because then the black-smith 'frost-sharpened' the shoes of the horse. Old Kit could just remember when the first mowing machine reached Kettlewell. 'Before that time, the grass was cut by scythe. My uncle stood six feet tall in his stockinged feet —and his scythe blade came up to his chin!'

When I first joined Harry Scott at Clapham, and collected material for *Dalesman* articles, I worked furiously, conscious that this was the tail-end of a long tradition. Only two dalesmen were uninterested in talking about the 'good old days'; one said they were not very good to him, and the other gave a great sigh and remarked, 'Nay, lad—what's ta want to go pokin' about in t'deeard past for?'

Chapter 6

A Romantic Interlude

Romance entered my life through dancing. I met Freda at the annual ball of the Craven Tenant Farmers' Association, held in the Town Hall at Skipton. It was the Big Band period of entertainment—the time of Geraldo and early Joe Loss. The strains of sweet and tuneful brass created a romantic sound that helped to off-set wartime memories and the dreariness of immediate post-war Britain. We had all become Americanised during the war, when Hollywood sent us a succession of romantic films, each one guaranteed to have a happy ending.

The Farmers' annual ball offered a respite from the wearying round of work and brought farm folk from a wide area, by bus, car and bike. Every self-respecting lad plastered his hair with Brylcreem and wore a suit, complete with braces and waistcoat. An unromantic aspect of that period was the style of shirt, with detachable collar, secured by studs. On farms, suits were not often worn and had to be draped over the backs of chairs, before a hot fire, to air. And, of course, there was a last-minute panic because someone had lost a collar stud.

For the young lady, taffeta was the thing. I recall that Freda had red taffeta, the dress extending to her ankles. Some girls went in for floral themes, but all had mini-handbags and silver shoes. A farmer's daughter would dash into the house from 'mucking out' in the shippons and become cocooned in her bedroom for an hour or so, to emerge resplendent—a dazzling butterfly. Father was inclined to tut-tut when he saw the make-up— a blue tinge above each eye and lips so red it looked as though there had been sudden, violent capillary action. Mother was eventually left alone among the debris created by now-departed sons and daughters.

The Town Hall was palatial compared with the wooden hut which served as a hall in many a Dales village—the hut, bought after the 1914–18 war, having been built as a barrack block for troops. I heard of a hut at Linton which was said to move under the surge of dancers during a Palais glide. I went with a few friends, Freda had arranged to go with her friends; we met, danced, chatted—and in due course met again. It was hardly 'Hollywood', but your average dalesman did not go in for undue sentiment and big bunches of flowers. My father's favourite story was of the Yorkshire couple who had been courting for 14 years when the girl said, 'Isn't it time we got wed?' He thought for a moment, then remarked, 'Who'd hev us?'

Skipton Town Hall was warm—and would become warmer still as over 200 dancers began to sweat. The vast floor was smooth—and would become smoother still after it had been sprinkled with powder and danced on for an hour or two. A most romantic atmosphere was created by an orb revolving high up, against the ceiling. It was composed of tiny mirrors, and when a spotlight rested upon it and the hall lights had been dimmed, the walls and ceiling were covered with a moving pattern of colourful blobs that would have put a peacock's tail to shame.

The annual Craven Tenant Farmers' Ball was an all-ticket do and a sell-out for weeks ahead of the date, unlike a village hop where you had plenty of space until the pubs closed and then had to fight for breath as well as space as a mass of dancers swirled, ebbed or flowed. A young man advanced on a young woman and asked her politely if she would care to dance. (An American shocked us by saying, 'Say—can I borrow your frame for a shuffle?') It was understood that the man would see the girl back to her chair. The territorial impulse led people to leave possessions like cardigans and jackets on their chosen seats and it would be a brave soul who took over such a seat while the tenant was dancing.

Our Big Band played all the old familiar tunes, and when we were not quick-stepping or foxtrotting to contemporary favourites, we went Down the Strand, sojourned at the Old Bull and Bush or proclaimed to the world in loud voices, while dancing, that My Girl's a Yorkshire Girl—Yorkshire Through and Through! Among the Tenant Farmers were families 'off t'tops', blinking at the bright lights and the unaccustomed crowd of people. I saw grey-haired men in crow-black suits, their shirts with the old-fashioned 'wing' collars, their footwear outmoded boots; young bucks set the fashion in dress suits and stimulated talk among the 'wallflowers', who remembered when Young Jack's father hadn't a penny to scratch his bottom on, and Young George's grandfather was—well, you know . . . And looks were exchanged. The 'you know' probably meant nothing more serious than being labelled a spendthrift and leaving a less than respectable sum in his will.

Freda was a farmer's daughter from Marton, 'way out west'. As the youngest of a family of five, she was able to seek employment outside the home acres. When I first knew her, she was a secretary at the Gargrave factory of Messrs Johnson and Johnson. Her route to work was circuitous. Setting off from home on a bike, and sometimes having a passenger in the young son of the estate agent, she pedalled to West Marton where, quite often, Mr Boothman the butcher was available to grab the bike and park it behind his shop while Freda dashed aboard the green-sided Laycock's bus for Broughton. From here, a works bus took her to Gargrave.

As in so much Dales activity in those days, events took on the character of a family get-together. At the Tenant Farmers' ball, the chatter was incessant—talk about tups and yows (male and female sheep), bee-asts (cattle), market prices, fertilisers and subsidies, plus the latest round-up of more personal information, such as who had 'run away' with whom. There was rather less hanky-panky than there is today . . .

The Lancers was announced. Most of the dancers withdrew from the floor, leaving it to the experts. Not only was it necessary to know how to dance The Lancers, but it would be danced with gusto, with loud whoops, exaggerated whirling movements and all the fury of a Cossack sabre dance. The Big Band struck up the opening chords —and away went the dancers on an unstoppable progress towards physical exhaustion. We noticed that most of the dancers were middle-aged, some with steel-grey hair at their temples, all with lean frames and muscles tuned up by much wielding of forks and shifting of milk kits on the farms. One or two had partly stripped for action. Some of the girls, who had agreed to take part 'just for devilment', regretted their decision when they were spun off their feet. One slipped from the grasp of the dancers and slid across the floor on her rump, coming to a halt again a knot of gossipers near the door.

Supper was served. More dancing followed. My progress in a progressive barn dance could be traced by the grunts of the ladies on whose tender feet I had trodden, for my dancing was untutored. In the cosy half-light, with the walls patterned with spinning forms and colours emanating from the orb that kept station high above us, like some satellite moon, the cares of the outer world could be forgotten.

On another day, Freda and I went to the pictures. We queued at the cinema on the wettest day of the year. Everyone had been soaked while waiting for tickets; everyone steamed in the warmth of the picture-house. I forget the name of the film, but recall that the walls ran with moisture and there must have been 85 per cent humidity. Items of outer clothing were being draped over the balcony to dry.

We went to various dances. Up at Tosside, the large wooden hut was heated by a stove which glowed red, sometimes white, taking the chill off the air before the dance began. The stove was in a central position and must surely impede the dancers. I had visions of third-degree burns or of taffeta shrivelling on touching the sides. My fears were groundless. A few minutes before the band struck up for the first dance, two men with iron bars advanced on the stove. A bar was slipped through holes on either side, and it was then lifted bodily and carried into the frosty night, to be left in a corner of the car park.

My first visit to Skelda Farm was on a winter day, with the crows in mournful voice, as though lamenting the loss of some of their brethren, victims of the gun of Freda's father, who couldn't abide crows for a reason that will be revealed later. Dead crows, tacked onto a fence, were dramatic evidence of his skill with a gun. He also shot foxes in winter, tracking them partly by sound, for it was in January that the courting took place, the howling of the vixen bringing forth a responsive bark from a nomadic dog fox.

The seventeenth-century farmhouse looked out over a green bowl, flanked by conifers and belts of rhododendrons. Straight ahead was the stable block of Old Gledstone. The mansion of the Roundells had been demolished on the instructions of the present owner of the estate, Sir Amos Nelson, one of the new-rich of the northern industrial towns. He had started out as a half-timer at the mill and had risen to the commercial heights through force of personality, hard work and business acumen. He and his first wife met a celebrated architect, Lutyens, on one of their cruises, and Lutyens persuaded Amos to commission a new house, which—of course—Lutyens would design and whose construction he would supervise.

Amos was aware of the architect's casual way with money: what mattered was the grand plan. He did his best to keep down costs, but they exceeded the budget figure. At the time the big new house was being built, in the 1920s, trade was on the down-turn. Amos kept his nerve. He was often critically short of money, though his circumstances suggested otherwise. Not until the coming of the

1939–45 war, and booming trade, did he regain his solvency.

Freda's family was among those who kept haytime machinery in the stable block—now a sad structure, battered by wartime use as a storage place for explosives. We stood in the brick-surfaced circular courtyard; we walked through the rooms where farriers had worked and on into the stables; we toured the upper galleries and marvelled at the affluence of past days. Old Gledstone had been obliterated except for the smaller cellars, where game had been hung.

Lady Nelson, Sir Amos's second wife, presided over the new Gledstone, with its lofty rooms, its staircases of alternating black and white marble steps, its chandeliers and a garden with terraces and lily-bedecked pool.

Something of the old spirit was maintained on Sunday mornings, when Lady Nelson and her staff entered the little old church by their own special door. She did her best to keep the Sabbath holy, and woe betide any tenant who hung out washing on a Sunday. She was none too keen on newspaper stories that mentioned Amos's humble upbringing. Yet she herself was the daughter of the estate agent and, as Freda's mother sometimes recalled, she had gone to the local school—wearing clogs.

Behind Skelda, fields extended to the low horizon and the landscape was dotted with outbarns. We walked to the highest point on the farm, where an Ordnance Survey triangulation station stood with a worthy panoramic view, extending from the limestone hills beyond the upper Ribble to the dark, dour hills of Bowland. Also in the view was Pendle, in Lancashire, to the south of which the famous group of witches had had their homes.

On that first day at Skelda, I watched Dad (Freda's father) and an older brother attending to the milking herd. Milking was carried out by machine, the power for which came from a 'donkey' engine, for mains electricity had not yet reached the Gledstone area. If the power failed, there was a clatter as the 'clusters' fell from the teats of the cattle. Gentle

Ayrshires dined on hay that held the scents of the summer hayfield, and especially of Yorkshire fog, that most aromatic of grasses. The hay-mow was solid and had to be attacked using a hay-knife, the food being delivered from a fodder-gang. While the milk was passing through the cooler and on through a piece of muslin into the kit, the men mucked out, the dung forming a rapidly-growing heap on one side of the barn, where it remained until the drying winds made the fields firmer to allow it to be spread. Men talked about good muck as a fertiliser; I had a theory that spreading the stuff was the most convenient way of getting rid of it.

Twice-a-day milking made a hole in the day. I marvelled at the tranquil state of the cows, which were tied up by the neck from November to May. Was it known for a cow to be so weary of the routine that it ran amok? I did not hear of such a beast. What on earth did a cow think about during the long hours spent in semi-darkness, eating, chewing the food and defecating, with no change of scene? The farmers had an unquestioning acceptance of their routine of milking stock and serving as lavatory attendants.

It was a very late tea that day; some bovine complication led to the men's return to the house later than usual. I found myself in a large living kitchen. On one side was the fireplace, part of a wrought-iron range that incorporated oven and wash-boiler. I was to see many such ranges in the Dales —Victorian affairs, foundry-made by the thousand but bearing the individual nameplates of those who sold them. In a farmhouse, before the coming of electricity, a fire was maintained the year through, even on the most blistering day, to provide hot water. The big iron kettle always had a song in its heart, and the boiler was kept well-filled with water that could be drawn off by tap. A kitchen range consumed vast quantities of wood and coal. Once a week, it received a coat of black-lead, which restored the gleam to its face.

The furniture in that kitchen was plain and substantial, having been handed down from generation to generation. I saw a large, square-topped table, a sideboard, a sofa of the horse-hair variety, two wooden chairs and two cane chairs, over the back of which black fleeces had been placed. A large clock with a mellow tick hung on one wall.

The better furniture was to be found in the parlour, beyond the grey-flagged passage, but on my first visit I was not to make the acquaintance of the parlour. It was also used for the reception of visitors, for Sunday hymn singing, with Mother on the piano (her favourite hymn tune was 'Rimington'), for Christmas parties and as a bolt-hole for courting couples.

Freda's mother quickly recovered from any embarrassment that my visit caused—and I was soon hearing about her Dales background. She was a Bushby from Kettlewell. Her grandmother was a member of the large family of Bell, who had filled many an acre of space in the graveyards of Wharfedale and Wensleydale. One of her ancestors, Matthew Bell, had been converted by the Mormons and, scarcely having left his native dale before, set off for Salt Lake City, taking ship from Liverpool to the mouth of the Missouri, crossing the plains where Indians were waiting to steal cattle and anything else that took their fancy, and arriving at the Mormon settlement by the Salt Lake when memories of Brigham Young were still fresh. (This much I discovered later, when a member of the family loaned me some letters that young Matthew Bell had written to his parents at Kettlewell.)

Dad had been born at Thornton-in-Craven and raised by an aunt who still lived at the family home at the edge of the moor. In due course I was to meet her on her 90th birthday, when she sat in state, her relatives around her. They paid tribute in words and gifts. She looked slowly from one to another and remarked, with spirit, 'I'll outlive t'lot on you!'

When Dad arrived, he slipped a good quality dark jacket over his shirt and after the introduction, awkwardly conducted—as is the way with men—reached for his trusty smoking pipe and soon clouded the air with strong fumes.

The jacket had been part of his wedding suit, purchased at Breare's shop in the Middle Row at Skipton. It refused to wear out.

It was a 'Sunday tea', featuring salmon, served as it was, turned out of the tin, and not mixed with breadcrumbs, as might be the case if only the immediate family was in attendance. This was an old Yorkshire custom. Salmon and salad; brown bread and scones; tinned pears and fresh cream; home-baked buns, fruit cake and lots of hot tea to drink—these were old Dales elements. After all, 'it's your stomach that 'ods your back up'.

The paraffin lamp disgraced itself. I was aware of dark smoke and of sooty deposits on the glass. Suddenly, the principal lighting had gone. We were left with the flickering light of the coal fire until someone cleaned the lamp, trimmed the wick and applied a match.

Dad's 12-bore gun rested on some brackets attached to one of the beams in the kitchen. He did not glory in killing beasties but acknowledged that sometimes it was necessary for the well-being of his stock. The foxes took his free-range hens. The rabbits—of which there were hundreds—kept the edges of his fields as short and fine as the green baize on a billiard table. The hens were also vulnerable to a predatory stoat. I was present when he shot the stoat. One mealtime, he left the kitchen and house doors open; his gun was propped against the doorway and a ladder reared against a high wall, beyond which lay the poultry run. When he heard the excited calling of hens, he rushed from his chair, grabbed the gun, climbed the ladder at a speed that would have brought a look of admiration to the face of a steeplejack —and despatched the stoat.

He was not callous. One day, he went for a walk with an old and faithful dog, which was now in pain. We heard the crack of gunshot, and he returned alone. The incident affected him deeply. He did not want to talk for the rest of the day.

I got to know some of the neighbouring farmers, especially one who wintered hoggs (young sheep) for a farmer in Swaledale. He was a poor neighbour, for he did not maintain his walls and hedges. The situation had its amusing moments. Freda and I, out walking, met him as he rammed a hogg onto the back seat of his new car. It was Eastertime, and this sheep had been missed during the gather. The other hoggs were already back in their upper Dales home. The farmer laughed.

'I reckon this sheep should be a good 'un,' he remarked. 'It came on a Sunday and it's going back o' Good Friday.'

Worse was to follow. His bull broke into one of Skelda fields and served a cow, an event that might have disrupted the breeding programme or introduced some undesirable elements into the herd. To be fair to the farmer, he apologised profusely and said he would do something about the fence. Dad did not reach a hasty decision. Months later, he said: 'I won't bother claiming compensation. That bull picked a cow which I was going to sell because it hadn't had a calf—and now that cow is "springing"!'

In those puritanical times, it was not unknown for a farmer to keep his family indoors on the day the bull arrived to serve some of the cows. I heard of a cunning bull that had the ability to slip its horns under a five-barred gate and lift it off its hinges; and of the aggressive animal which, when it decided to go for a cross-country expedition, simply fell heavily against any gates in its path. In most cases, the gates were immediately shattered.

* * *

Courting had its conventions. It began with one-night-a-week meetings that ended early (particularly early, if I went to Skelda, for the last bus was at 9 p.m.). A second night might then be arranged, but young couples did not see each other daily, as appears to be the case nowadays. We chuckled at the experience of a girl whose mother, an elderly widow, enjoyed 'courting night'. She had an afternoon nap and spent much time donning her best clothes. She selected the best chair in the living room and remained with the couple until it was time for the young man to go.

The young people found this frustrating. One night a tremendous clattering sound was heard. Neighbours thought the lad's patience must have come to an end and he was hitting the old lady with some object, but his aggression was directed to useful ends. Not being able to stand another minute under the withering gaze of his future mother-in-law, he decided to mend the sofa and, turning it upside down, he set to work on it with a hammer!

If Dad was not suffering from a cold—and he was 'a poor hand at suffering', placing his head in his hands and sighing loudly at five-minute intervals—he could be entertaining. There was perhaps a score of amusing stories in his repertoire. He told of Moonlight Jack, the waller. When he had caught up to date and no gaps in walls remained, he went out on moonlit nights and pulled down some more. I heard of the two cattle dealers—brothers—who attended an auction mart but attempted to do the dealing without having to pay a commission to the company. So one brother haggled about the purchase of a cow. Half an hour later, the other brother sidled up to him and whispered:

'Hev you got it bought?'

'No.'

'Well, hurry up—I've just sold it.'

Dad kept a pig. All surplus food was tossed into the sty, to be converted into toothsome flesh by the snorting, snuffling animal. Dad's sausages were famous, for he used pork unadulterated with breadcrumbs—a wartime ruse —and with some seasoning of his own devising. To one brought up on Co-op sausages, and having a good appetite, it astonished me that just two of Dad's sausages were so filling. He told of the farmer who fitted a chute to the sty so that he could throw in food without wasting time. One day he noticed the food was piling up. He looked over the wall. The pig had been dead for three days!

In spring, we walked across the still chilled fields with a dog and rounded up the heavily-pregnant ewes, driving them to a croft near the farm, where they might be handy during the night, for Dad intended to cat-nap on the horse-hair sofa in the kitchen and make his rounds with a storm lantern at times during the night. I have mentioned that he hated the carrion crow. The bird is intelligent and opportunistic. It does well in lambing time, dining on the afterbirth, and is always ready to attack the weakly or ailing lamb. We found lambs which faced the world with eyeless sockets, because of the visitation of crows.

New-born lambs that just lacked stamina for a long trek back to the farm were carried. I look back with pleasure on springtime evenings when the meadows were banded with yellow light from a low-slung sun; on the feel of a lamb's rib-case as I carried the mite; of how powerful was the heart that thumped the blood around that as-yet-slack little body; and of how earnest was the mother ewe as she followed, bleating urgently.

Dad had a way with lambs. He knew all about the subterfuge of skinning a dead lamb and slipping the skin over the back of an orphan in the hope that the ewe, familiar with the scent, would accept the stranger. I would enter the kitchen after a cold, wet night to find a lamb in a box before the fire, losing the chill from its joints. Another lamb would be in the process of being fed with milk warmed dramatically when Dad plunged a red-hot poker into it.

Uncle Fred called at the farm. He was as tall and gangling as Dad and Aunt Annie were small, but all three were lean and 'lish'. Uncle Fred's wife came from Ulverston—and never let us forget it. We gathered that Ulverston was famous for two things—a dummy lighthouse set on a hill and Stan Laurel, of Laurel and Hardy fame; he had been born in the town and it was a shame they had not created a monument to him. Fred's wife came to the Dales via the famous old hiring fair at Ulverston. Many a lass who was hired for domestic work on a farm did well for herself and married the farmer's son, eventually presiding over the farm and producing Yorkshire/Lancashire offspring.

When Uncle Fred was left on his own—which is a roundabout way of saying that his wife had died—a great silence fell on his house and he embarked on a period of globe-trotting. It went on for years—until he was in his early 90s. His photograph album gave a pictorial account of flights to America via the North Pole, voyages in merchant ships down the African coast and excursions to the Antipodes.

He still managed to keep up his local associations. Each Sunday, from his new bungalow home at Bradley, he sauntered forth—on foot—to ring the bells at Broughton Church, across the valley. He contrived to do this by holding one rope and wrapping the others round arms and legs. Each Whit Tuesday, he was at the Sermons in Horton-in-Craven Chapel, with a rapt look on his face. Uncle Fred was not concentrating on what was being said: he was preoccupied by food. I was invited to preside over the Sermons. The weather on Whit Tuesday was invariably fine: this year, the conditions were outstanding. The sun had leapt into the sky as though anxious to get on with the day, and it had no competition from clouds. Freda and I caught the bus to Horton lane end, and walked up a road between hedges that were spring-fresh and clamorous with small birds. Buses from Barnoldswick deposited more worshippers at the end of the lane; gossiping groups walked briskly to where a few houses overlooked the minor road. This was Horton, which was normally 'busy' only in the sense of being curious about other people's affairs. It was said that a local farmer stopped strangers and asked them where they were going.

Horton Chapel, a relic of the old Independency, was an outstanding survival of its type. The Chapel was staunchly independent, its members having a direct line to God. Uncarpeted stairs led to a gallery that should not be visited by sufferers of vertigo. The organ was up here, its pipes set in an ornate frame and its large size reflecting the local passion for a 'good sing'. The pulpit seemed to occupy a quarter of the building and rose in a glory of ornate woodwork. I climbed the steps with the two ministers who had agreed to deliver the Sermons. My vision was impeded by the front of the gallery, which seemed only a dozen feet away. In the centre, and also at eye level, was a large clock. It was said that the grey-haired man sitting immediately above the clock coughed when a service had been in progress for an hour, and that the discomfort in his throat would produce further coughs and rasping sounds until the last hymn was announced. To keep an eye on all the worshippers, it would have been necessary to have a neck made of India rubber. I had to bend my neck back to behold the worshippers in the gallery, and to peer downwards —down, down, down—to see those who had decided to sit at ground level. Down there, too, was the main reason why the Chapel was packed one Tuesday in May. Woe betide the minister who spoke for too long; for the meal awaiteth. Horton Chapel cherished until recent times one of the glories of Nonconformity—the outstanding catering abilities of its womenfolk.

I would see Uncle Fred, looking up at the pulpit with a pious expression, yet within arms' length of him was the nearest trestle table with its load of goodies, covered with freshly-laundered white cloths. If his eyes did stray from the speaker, it was to reassure himself that preparations for ʕChapel tea were going on smoothly—that there was a murmuration from the boiler in the next little room, where water was being heated up for tea.

We sang. We prayed. We listened to first-class sermons. We waited until the last speaker said, 'And so, friends, that leads me to my last point . . .' Then the last hymn was announced, benediction pronounced, and the shuffling began as positions were claimed on the chairs and forms about the tables. Matronly women with fresh, smiling faces and newly-donned pinafores, appeared with huge teapots.

That was when Uncle Fred came into his own. He did not rush, as did the inexperienced, when the cloths were taken away and the feast appeared to view. He did not grab—as did the children, working their way furiously from sand-wiches to scones, from scones to cream cakes, from cream cakes to trifle. He did not stuff his mouth with good food, like Eskimos gathered around a newly-dead whale.

Uncle Fred knew from previous years what the ladies of the area would have prepared from their old-fashioned recipe books, working with farm-fresh butter, eggs and milk in old-fashioned kitchens. While the sermons were on, he had planned his strategy. He chewed every mouthful a dozen times. He paused frequently. He was the first to start eating; his champing and tea-drinking extended from the first sitting to the second and, maybe an hour-and-a-half later, he stood up, completely satisfied—and wondered what he might make for supper!

The months sped by, and it was haytime. For Freda and me, 'courting' could be forgotten for a month until a crop of hay had been safely gathered in. Dad rapped the barometer with the fervour of a woodpecker tapping out a drum-signal in spring. He no longer made an effort to be humorous: there was nothing funny about a slow start to haytime. He periodically sighed—and reached for his favourite pipe, sending smoke signals to the Weather Clerk. I recalled —but not to him—his story of the old farmer who had a barometer that was 'set fair'. Outside his home, the rain fell as though from a celestial hosepipe. The old man took the barometer from the wall; he took it into the yard, held it up and said, 'Sithee!' (Translation: 'Have a look!')

The weather was feckless for a few more days. Farmers awoke early and scanned the sky for a sign—a patch of blue 'big enough to patch a Dutchman's trousers'. I looked up a dialect dictionary and was impressed by the number of Dales words relating to the weather—glishy (for one of those gleaming mornings when the bright weather does not last long); clashy (for the stormy weather that soaks a person to the skin); packy (for a day on which the sky is well filled with clouds); and snizy (a raw day).

A drying wind swept away the last tatters of cloud. Farm folk set to work in the meadows, under the blue vault of a cloudless sky.

Chapter 7

'Cuckoo Town'

Freda and I were married on a golden day in early September. It was a 'mixed marriage' (Anglican/Methodist) but took place at St Peter's Church, East Marton. The vicar, Canon Chance, had baptised and confirmed Freda. Her initials appeared with others on one side of the organ where, in days past, the organ-blower had whittled away with a knife as a form of occupational therapy.

The organist was a wealthy businessman who lived in the parish and had always wanted to play at a village wedding. Transport for my Skipton relatives was provided by Mr Hey, of Silver Star buses, Carleton, though he struck a hard bargain—£3 for the day, driver included. The bells were rung by anyone who had the energy, which was the local way.

In the mellow autumn sunshine, St Peter's looked half as old as time. With my best man, Trevor, I did as I had been instructed and sat down half an hour before service time. We stared at the altar, then at the pulpit; we memorised details of the figures on the stained glass windows and began to count the organ pipes. We seemed to have run out of time and were halfway through eternity.

Harry Scott and Mrs B were in the congregation. I heard Mrs B whispering loudly. A woman said testily (to her husband, I presumed), 'Well, you should have gone before we set off!' Silence again. We resumed our counting of the organ pipes. The bride arrived, late as per custom—though not many brides are 20 minutes late.

The driver of the Silver Star bus inquired anxiously about the venue for the reception, having already overshot the church. We were booked in at the Old Vicarage, a wooden structure behind the church at Gisburn. Freda and I had gone along with Dad to order the meal. He was not out for a bargain that day, unlike one of his friends who bartered over the meal, eventually settled on a price that scarcely covered the restaurant owner's costs, and then said, triumphantly, 'How much will it be if I fetch my own ham?' Freda was the last of the family to be married. Dad actually made a speech, which took everyone by surprise. He said, 'I went to Skipton auction mart on Monday. A farmer came up to me and said, "I hear tell thou's gettin' sold up o' Saturday."'

The bus took the guests on to Freda's home, where the presents were displayed. At least a third of them were useful, the rest being decorative, including a purple vase and a circular mirror that looked from a distance like a dartboard. Then we were whisked away to the railway station at Skipton in a car that had been attended the whole time. No one had had the opportunity to lift the bonnet and place a couple of kippers on the engine. The driver had discouraged someone who wanted to tie a string of tin cans to the back bumper.

The steam-hauled train for Glasgow thundered into the station. We stood at a window, in a storm of confetti. The train drew away from the platform. We found ourselves in a first-class carriage, which explained why it was empty when so many other compartments were packed with people. The ticket-collector looked at the confetti and our third-class tickets, clipped the tickets and said, with great verbal economy, 'Wedding present.' The train clattered northwards. We honeymooned at Oban. Our married life began in Mrs B's front room at Austwick with some wedding presents, including the purple vase, and £48 in the bank . . . We had hoped to make it £50 but I was still incinerating cigarettes by the yard.

We had settled in a village that enjoyed the distinction of

being 'daft'. Austwick's second name was 'Cuckoo Town', a reference to an ancient tale of some of the local men who, associating the arrival and departure of the cuckoo with the weather—and believing the bird was responsible for all the warm days they enjoyed—reasoned that if they could keep a cuckoo in the village the winter through, then they would retain the good weather. So they waited until a cuckoo went to roost in a tree, and during the night they built a tall wall around it. There was universal disappointment when, at first light, the bird simply flew over the wall and departed.

We took up residence at a time when most of the people of Austwick had been born in the locality. Sally Pritchard was called 'auntie' by the village children, and it was not just a courtesy title. She was auntie-in-law to most of them. Will Pritchard, her husband, couldn't abide 'craws'—mainly carrion crows, though the term included rooks, which nested freely in the big trees by the church. (One of the trees was called the 'whittle tree', after a small butcher's knife that was hung there, being the only knife in the village at that time. If someone wanted a knife, they went to the tree. If the knife was already being borrowed, they went around the village shouting, 'Whittle to t'tree!' Or so it was related in yet another daft story . . .)

Will Pritch, as he was known, regularly stood up in the Annual Assembly and declared, 'What about them craws?' He was never fussy at which point in the meeting he brought up the old topic and was usually ruled out of order. Some of the local naturalists winced. The 'craws' did not nest in peace, for Will was usually out and about at first light with his trusty gun. He heralded the dawn, and startled a few rooks, by discharging his gun in the general direction of the trees. If he heard anyone approaching, he would slip the gun under cover of the bus shelter.

Our butcher, Norman, told me a somewhat bloodthirsty story about a whittle. It seems that his father took on a new apprentice. On the first morning, he said (teasingly) to the

lad, 'Tak this whittle, catch yon sheep and cut its throat.'
The lad protested. 'Well, then—catch the sheep for me.'
But the sheep did not want to be caught. By the time he had
a grip on its horns, the lad was hot and bothered. Dragging
the animal to the butcher, he said, 'Where's that blooming
knife?'

In 1952, when my wife and I had been married for a few
weeks, a seventeenth-century cottage became available for
rent. I went to see the owner on a wild winter evening. He
opened the door of his house and peered at my sleet-
silvered figure standing on the step. He agreed to the
tenancy of his cottage and then, having built up a balance of
good will, added, 'Will you help me with haytime next year?'
Of course I would! In any case, haytime, when considered
on that late November day, was far into the future. (Ten
minutes later—or so it seemed—the farmer turned up at
the door of the cottage and said, with verbal economy, 'It's
haytime.' And so it was.)

Our cottage was part of a row that traditionally was
occupied by Methodists. Living next door was dear old Mrs
Handby and her brother, Harry Holden, a great waller in
his time who, though of an advanced age, would set off to
the market on foot—almost 10 miles, there and back—even
if he made only one purchase. Mrs Preece, in the end
cottage, summoned me when she had a blocked drain or a
new bulb was needed. She turned on her living room light
and the wireless as she arose and all three remained active
until bedtime. The last time I changed a bulb—it was a 40
watt bulb—she looked displeased. 'It hasn't been in long,'
she announced. 'How long? I inquired. She 'reckoned up'.
How time flies. The bulb had been used continually for six
years!

Jimmy/Johnny, the farming brothers who had the field
behind our cottage, turned up periodically. Otherwise their
fine cattle divided their time between grazing, chewing the
cud and looking through our back windows, which had
been barred to prevent a hundredweight or two of living
flesh from descending onto the hearth. Nathan Booth, a

retired farmer, passed on his daily walk. He was a tough old chap. I heard that one day, when he was hand-milking, he winced, felt a tooth, pronounced it was bad and promptly went into the house and removed it with some pliers. He returned to his milking, winced again and said to the neighbour who had been talking to him, 'Heck! I've got t'wrong tooth.' He promptly went back into the house and yanked out the offending tooth.

In the Dales, two classes of people could be found —Farmers and Others. This, at least, was the impression I received from knowing Fred, a near neighbour who was one of the former. He was very proud of his status. Now and again, when a name cropped up in conversation, Fred would observe, 'He's a farmer.' Nothing further need be said.

Fred had had a 'sparse' upbringing. There were many mouths to feed, his father having had two successive wives and an ultra-large family. Yet Fred had persevered and saved and worked and attained the distinction of being a Farmer—a proper Farmer, owning all the land he could see from his farmhouse. Every farmer wanted to leave enough 'brass' to impress his friends and neighbours. I had a feeling, from the look on Fred's face when wills were mentioned, that this public aspect of his own financial affairs would be as good for him as an effusive line on a tombstone.

When he retired to town, he expected a daily report from his son at the farm. Fred was sometimes upset by the newfangled ideas that were introduced, and he would say to his son, 'It's aw reet as long as thou keeps t'cart on t'wheels.' (He also used this expression with a bemused, city-bred vicar who wanted to introduce some radical new idea to the church.) The son managed the farm well. A much better cart was on order!

Fred liked others to know he was a farmer, so when he had mown the lawn, he trimmed the edges with a pair of sheep-clippers. As in most Dales families, he was known in later life as 'Dad'. The old name, used when the kids were young, persisted into old age. By the same token, Fred's wife was 'our Mother'. We once borrowed a camp bed from them. He helped me carry it downstairs and, seeing his wife standing at the bottom, turned and said, in a gentle voice, 'Get thi fat lump out of t'way, our Mother.' She moved, with a smile.

Modern gadgets were beyond him. He 'could make nowt of yon telephone in t'kiosk—there's just a high-pitched burring note.' We allowed him to receive calls on our telephone. Once or twice, his family rang. Fred could not imagine anyone using the telephone socially, so he would stalk across the living room, pick up the receiver and, expecting details of some calamity, bark: 'Now what?'

Farmers prided themselves on being 'careful'. They remembered the grim years, when 'brass' was tight and the local grocer, when making up an order, would not give a grain of sugar too many and also 'nipped a currant in two' to get the precise weight. Farm men usually inquired, if they were to hire, whether a prospective employer 'kept a good table' or asked, 'Is it a good jock place?' Mrs Fred was a great cook. Fred himself chuckled at the remembrance of one farmer's wife who made up lettuce sandwiches for the haytime meal. 'One bit o' lettice leaf in each sandwich!' reported their farm man. 'I put her to shame, though. When she wasn't looking, I stuck a tuft o' grass in each sandwich. After that we got egg as well!'

Only once had Fred been outwitted in a deal, and he hated to be reminded of it. Years before, he had bought a horse from a man with whom he had never been on especially friendly terms. The pre-sale discussion had been long and wearying. Fred had run his hand over the horse's hocks, and insisted on it being run up and down a field so that he might study its action. He looked at its eyes, he peered into its ears and even ran his fingers through its mane and tail. Eventually the deal was done. Not long afterwards, he noticed with dismay that the horse hung its head. He could not get the animal to stand 'proper': it looked positively dejected.

He took the horse back to the farmer who had owned it.

'This hoss isn't reight,' he began.

'What's up wi' it?' asked the farmer.

Fred said, 'It wean't hold its head up.'

The farmer's moment had arrived, and he savoured every delicious second. Fred had often taken a rise out of him. Making sure there was another farmer nearby so that the tale would go its rounds, he said, 'I'll tell thee what's wrang wi' yon hoss, Fred.'

'I wish thou would,' said Fred.

The farmer smiled. 'It wean't hold its head up because of pride—thee get it paid for!'

In that household, everything related to farming. Fred became a grandfather and my wife asked Fred's wife about the new arrival. It was a huge baby, weighing over nine pounds at birth.

'Is it good at night?'

'Nay,' said the farmer's wife. 'It's allus crying; and when it cries it's just like a gurt calf bawling!'

In February, as an easterly wind brought flurries of snow and t'owd yows sheltered in the lee of the walls, the annual Herd Letting was held in the Parish Hall. In February, the pulse of the farming year beat slowly. It was, in effect, midwinter, for a farmer was anxious if he did not have at least half his hay crop left at this time. He knew that in February and March, when many townsfolk were looking for signs of the coming spring, stock was well into the 'starvation' period, the cattle indoors, the sheep wandering across a landscape on which the vegetation was sere, short of protein.

I much enjoyed the Herd Letting. The name means 'shepherd letting', and years before the main business was considering tenders from likely men for caring for sheep on the big stinted pastures of Moughton, Oxenber and Long Scar (Ingleborough). Farmers turned out as many sheep as there were 'stints' or 'gaits' associated with their holdings.

To assess the area of grazing, using the term 'acre' was a pointless exercise, for much of the land was covered with outcropping limestone.

Now the farmers were resigned to doing the work themselves. They met to discuss the letting of Little Wood on Oxenber, one of the few tracts of indigenous woodland in the area. They talked about walls. They rebuked anyone who might have turned out too many sheep. A story was told of the man who habitually drove onto one of the pastures too many sheep. Eventually, he was persuaded to reduce the numbers. On the following day, another farmer saw a lad bringing down sheep. He counted them. The number was just below the maximum allowed. He complimented the lad on the quality of the sheep. 'It's nowt compared with t'big batch I browt down yesterda',' was the reply.

We gathered in the Supper Room, with an open fire and forms for seating. William Fell, the secretary, sat at a card table on which reposed an ancient calf-bound minute book. The first entry, made in the year before the Battle of Waterloo was fought, was in stylish copperplate. The last, recent entry, was brief; the ink came from a ballpoint pen!

I was fascinated to hear from one of the farmers that Austwick Moss, a stretch of original marshland, and a prime haunt of Yorkshire botanists, was once divided into 'dales'. A map of 1870 showed 30 tracts of land, associated with the neighbouring farms. Before coal was being brought to this area in large quantities, peat was an inexpensive fuel in great demand.

We were living at Austwick at the time when local farming was being transformed through mechanisation. For seven successive summers I enjoyed a spell of haymaking, helping our landlord and Frank Lambert. That first year was memorable because we worked with a horse and cart. The horse was called Peggy and I was amazed at her intestinal activity as revealed by the frequent passage of air as she drew the cart twixt hayfield and barn. 'She's a grand 'un,' said Frank.

Frank typified the old-time dalesman. He was born and reared in North Ribblesdale; he remembered the days when a farm man—as he once was—was not encouraged to enter the farmhouse except for meals and at bedtime. On cold mornings, he warmed his hands on the backs of cows standing in the shippons.

His vocabulary took in many old Pennine terms. When he was in the midst of a hectic round of jobs, he was 'amanghands'. He was fond of using terms that were unfamiliar to me, and so the back door of the cart he used for muck-spreading and then for haymaking was a 'heck'. In the hayfield, he told me to 'kem t'cart down'. I did—on the following night, after I had checked with a dialect dictionary of about 1840 and discovered that 'kem' meant 'to comb'. He had been asking me to remove loose hay from the cart with my rake.

Frank worked with a slow deliberation. I never knew him get cross. At the time I knew him, he was 'getting on', about 60 years old, I reckon, and so he no longer tried to impress anyone with his strength. It was left to Fred or myself to fork up hay from rows and lift it onto the cart which Peggy dutifully hauled, working purely on spoken commands. I once held up a lump of grass that was still green; it had not experienced the drying power of sun or breeze. 'What shall I do with this, Frank?'

'Put it in t'cart—when it gets in t'barn, it'll help hay to sweat!' I shuddered to think what Freda's father would say of such behaviour.

Haytime was in late June or July. The grass that was mown had not been stimulated into lusty growth by modern fertilisers, but was responding to good muck, plus a bit of basic slag and a few loads of lime. Such grass was easy to kill, and there was a satisfying rustle about it. (I would never have imagined, in the 1950s, that the remorseless march of time would bring into existence a machine that picked up silage in a roll, silage that was later slipped into a large plastic bag; and that this work could be done when it was raining, with the result that when the bag was opened at least five gallons of water would pour out.)

In that first summer at Austwick, I heard a corncrake in one of William Fell's meadows. It was the last corncrake to appear in a district where once the species was common. Before our landlord mowed his and Frank's meadows with a machine attached to his Ferguson tractor—the 'little grey Fergy'—the summer breezes created patterns as they swept over acres of grass and abundant wild flowers.

Most of the work was done by hand. We turned the swathes, rowed up and loaded carts with only rake and fork to help us. The shafts raised innumerable 'water blisters' on the tender parts of my hands. And as we worked, curlews dipped and called. The harvest being quite late, we had not caught their young half-grown and helpless.

When the time came for the hayfield meal, known as 'drinkings', Frank told stories of the old haytimes, when teams of men with scythes felled the meadow grasses. They talked of 'bat' (the distance the mower moved forward) and of 'breead' (which was the breadth of his cut). He showed me a wooden object called a 'strickle'. About the size of a truncheon, but four-sided, it was attached to the scythe shaft and helped to maintain the balance as the implement was being used. Its chief purpose lay in sharpening a scythe blade. Before haytime, farm men were sent to moorland tarns to collect 'scythe sand', which was hard but fine. The strickle was pitted with small holes and, when in use, was smeared with bacon fat, then dusted with sand. The sand worked its way into the tiny holes and was held firmly there by the grease. The abrasive surface was ideal for giving a scythe blade a new edge.

'Drinkings' were always welcome. We ate the sandwiches, scones and cake; the hayfield insects, especially the horseflies (clegs) ate us. It was bad in the evening, when the midges took flight and the swarms were as dense as smoke; they irritated us by their biting, and they almost drove poor Peggy crazy. It was said that if you killed a midge, 1,000 of its friends would attend the funeral.

Next year, Peggy was absent. The 'little grey Fergy' tractor reigned supreme. I asked Frank what had happened to Peggy. He replied, quietly, as though hoping I would not hear him, 'I sold her for meat.'

Chapter 8

On Four Wheels

Harry Scott had had a brief career as a motorist. The car engine was so temperamental that—like Mrs B's petrol-powered mowing machine—once started it was best not to let it stall. When taking the family to Skipton to do some shopping, he would draw up in the High Street and stand by the car, keeping the engine running. Dorothy Scott made a round of the shops and they drove back home with an overheated engine. In the 1930s, not many people had cars. Many a farmer went to market on the bus or had a motor-bike.

I knew nothing about the technical aspects of cars and had a fellow-feeling for the Dales farmer who returned a new car to the garage with the remark, 'It's not rattlin' reight.' My first vehicle, a Ford saloon, was purchased second-hand, though on reflection—and considering its sad condition it might have been tenth-hand. It was two-tone, black and rust. I drove the car to our local garage under the bemused stare of locals who knew a bit about vehicles. The mechanic could not wait to inspect my car and joyfully reported its faults, including, if I remember aright, a crack in the chassis, piston 'slap' and tappet rattle. 'And by the way, the engine mountings are corroded. That engine waddles about as you drive . . .'

In our early married life, we used the Pennine bus to visit the market town of Settle or for outings to the cinema in Ingleton on a Saturday evening. At times, walking was a necessity, not just a weight-reducing exercise. One hoped, when walking far at night, for a full moon. On cloudy,

moonless nights, a local man used to say, 'The village
lantern's gone out.' The need for a car arose with the arrival
of a family—David in 1954 and Janet in 1957. There was a
limit to what a pram would hold, though in the carless days
it was pushed up hill, down dale. We ventured into places
where—not having caterpillar tracks—that pram had to be
carried.

With a wife and two bairns, and next-to-nothing in the
bank, I had had to go for a bargain. The mechanic gave me
some free advice about the car: sell it! I must pick a rainy
day. 'There's nowt like a film o' watter on a car to mak it
sparkle.' I must park it so that the good side of the chassis
was close to a wall. 'Then t'poor begger you're selling it to
won't see t'crack when he looks under t'car from t'other
side. And . . .' He rambled on. I had no intention of selling
the car, even when the driving seat collapsed and was
replaced by a second-hand one twice as heavy. I had to
have a new floor installed. One of Harry Scott's relatives
obliged me by fitting a floor. He made a lovely job of it, and
replaced the carpeting.

A few months later, I was driving home down Wharfedale in heavy rain when my seat began to topple. The new
floor, of some composition material, had not stood up well
to the overwhelmingly damp Dales climate. It had become
quite soft and yielded under the weight of the heavy seat. I
drove to the nearest joiner, contriving to find a central
position in the car, with the gear lever between my legs.
Glancing down, I saw the hole in the floor and the road-
way passing as a grey blur beneath. When the joiner had
recovered from his amusement, he put in some quite
ordinary floor-boarding.

The car enabled me to extend my range—to reach parts of
the Dales that other forms of transport could not reach.
Such as Swaledale.

To reach it from Clapham meant travelling against the
grain of the landscape. My road unfolded as long, open
stretches—by Gearstones to Newby Head and down
Widdale to Wensleydale; thence over the Buttertubs,

snow-streaked until well into spring, to meet the valley of the Swale between Thwaite and Muker. I beheld Ribblehead viaduct, its 24 arches draped across the valley like a Victorian cobweb, and my eyes quested for Wold Fell, the source of Gayle Beck, longest tributary of the Ribble. This ever-leaking Fell, which is capped by limestone, also sends becks northwards to join the Rawthey and eastwards to the Ure.

The Buttertubs Pass, a highway in a literal sense, takes its name from several limestone shafts. It was near them that I stopped my wheezing car so that it might cool off. From the moor came the whistle of a golden plover. The fluty aria of a ring ouzel—the white-bibbed 'mountain blackbird'—could be heard in the echo-chamber of the ravine. A gamekeeper I know calls the ring ouzel 'our northern nightingale'. (At Tailbrigg, above Mallerstang, I found a pair nesting on a ledge in a pothole.)

A walker I met near Muker quoted from the local song, beginning:

> Beautiful Swaledale, land of rest;
> Beautiful Swaledale, I love thee the best.
> The land it is set in a cultivate style;
> The extension of Swaledale is twenty long mile.

Twenty long mile! 'Until I came to Swaledale I'd no idea how long a mile really is. Anyway, it was only my feet that complained. The rest of me enjoyed the walk.' When walking from Grinton up the hill to the youth hostel, a local man, surprised that anyone should walk about the Dales for pleasure, had remarked, 'Haven't ye got a home?' I had not been in Swaledale for half an hour when someone referred to 't'dale', in such a homely way I imagined that a family spirit prevailed throughout.

Mrs Nancy Parker, at Muker post office, showed me a peat turf, cut from a local moor, which had been given her to remind her of the time when she spent summer days on the moors, peating. 'A good peat fire takes a lot of beating,' she said. 'It burns away to a very fine dust, and it's comfortable to sit beside in the winter-time . . . We got our coal from the pits on Tan Hill, and this was a boon when there were strikes or wars. The coal wasn't of good quality, but it kept our grates warm. Tan Hill coal and peat from the moors have been a blessing to the folk living at the top end of the dale.'

I heard about Muker Band, formed in 1879, and about Neddy Dick, a musical celebrity at Keld. He kept in his cottage a battered harmonium, and a stand holding over a score of bells taken from old grandfather clocks. The pride and wonder of his collection was a 'rock band'. It was made up of 'musical' stones collected from the becks and streams of Upper Swaledale. Neddy was one of innumerable local nicknames: his real name was Richard Alderson.

As usual, I was regaled with lots of amusing stories —part of the 'small change' of Dales life. Dick Guy told me how an old Dales character, having come close to the end of his life, was given help and companionship by neighbours and friends, who sat up with him at night. 'Mary Anne's turn came round. She went to the bedroom and saw that the old man was comfortable. He seemed contented and she decided that she would snatch a little sleep. Pulling out the couch, she lay upon it and draped a rug across her body. She was just ready for sleep when the old man called out, 'Mary—is thoo sittin' up wi' me, or is Ah sittin' up wi' thee?'

He also told me about Nanny Peacock, who kept a local inn. She was asked if she ever went to Chapel, and replied, 'No, Ah doan't—but Ah respect those 'at does.' Yet everyone conformed to the Sunday observance rule: only vital jobs should be done. Before Muker received a piped water supply, the locals carried water from a small spout near the bridge. On Saturday evening, it was always busy. People carried as much water as they would need until Monday.

Those were the days when the native population was predominant. The 'holiday cottage' was uncommon, and 'off-comers' were simply those who came for holidays in summer. Swaledale was the home and workplace of families like the Calverts, who provided blacksmiths at Gunnerside for over 200 years. When I motored over in my little old Ford, the present generation—father and son—still laboured at the anvil, which rested on a roller that had been used at one of the lead mines. The weathered door had been scorched where the Calverts had made 'proofs' of stamps they had made for the mines. Willie Calvert remembered the mining days, when gruvers (miners), smelters and dressers could be seen walking to and from their workplaces. These men were old at fifty because of the hazardous work. 'I have heard of men working in places where a candle wouldn't burn because of the foul air. Many men got chest trouble. The different mines closed almost at the same time, and families with girls usually went to the cotton mills in Lancashire. Families with boys headed for Durham, where there was work for willing men in the coal pits.'

The mining theme was sustained by Miss Ruth Alderson. She told me of men who went off along the 'gruvers' trods' to mine lead, while their womenfolk ran the little fellside farms and brought up their quite large families. 'Many of the men never saw the village in daylight when winter came along—except on Sundays, of course. Some of the mines were three miles away, in difficult country.' Her father, a bootmaker, once took up a job as 'watcher' at the Engine House in Sir George Dennis's mine. 'He had to travel underground for two miles to get there! When Sir George came to Gunnerside, the local brass band met him. He liked them to play: "The Girl I left Behind Me."'

Thomas Armstrong, the novelist, had written *Adam Brunskill*, a long novel about local lead-mining. He welcomed me to his home, a late Georgian building called Lawn House, standing near the river at Low Row. We chatted in a room that was lagged with books and rendered lively and colourful by the paintings of Fred Lawson. In 18 months of research into lead-mining, he had gathered half a million words in reference notes: his novel was an impressive 260,000 words long. It was said of Thomas Armstrong that every time he wrote a book, he learnt a new trade or profession!

This particular Swaledale journey ended at Low Row with talk of death. Ernest Bagshaw, joiner and undertaker, with premises at Reeth, remembered when his hearse was drawn by two black horses. He kept a record of all the black horses in the district, and could draw on three pairs if desired. (As we spoke, I thought of the old Corpse Road down the dale—the route taken by the daleheaders to the nearest consecrated ground, which was at Grinton. The bodies were in wicker baskets and carried for miles at a time.)

Ernest took me back in his memory to the days when a funeral card, black-edged, with printed information about the deceased, was sent out to relatives and friends. Funeral cakes were made, these being 'round, cut across the middle and folded, wrapped in good quality white paper and sealed with black wax'. Port or sherry were available before the funeral, and afterwards—at the special meal— everyone tucked in to a worthy repast, featuring ham and beef.

* * *

In later years Matthew Cherry was my guide to remote parts of Swaledale. He was a most genial and informative companion on outings to places like Swinnergill, Gunnerside Gill and, of course, Old Gang, with its ruined smelt mill and two rows of pillars of native stone that had once supported a thatched roof and served as a peat store. After each excursion, we returned to his house, where Mrs Cherry provided a substantial Dales tea.

Our path to Swinnergill lay across the edge of Ivelet Common. This way strode the gruvers, stopping now and again for a smoke, drawing the fumes from black twist up the brittle stems of clay pipes. The narrow strip of beaten earth was now a major route for hill sheep. The path was littered with their hard, round droppings that did little to compensate the ground for all the goodness the sheep had drawn from it while grazing. We were in high limestone country. The cattle grazed sweet grass and the rainwater had an aversion to running on the surface for long, but soon found a crack and went underground. Lapwings wailed a warning to their young, which snuggled into the reed beds and kept their heads down. Where walls and grey screes were abundant, the stean-chat (wheatear) punctuated the day with whistles and chacks.

Soon we were in the mining area, peering into adits, where the air was dark and damp and the mortarless walls were festooned with ferns. We saw a fine show of spring sandwort, a plant tolerant to lead. The white flowers were massed like daisies on a lawn, marking precisely the areas disturbed for mining.

At Swinnergill, my eye was captivated by a bridge. This was no ordinary bridge. Finely-masoned, of single span, it sprang from cliff to cliff across the deep bed of the beck. Anyone crossing it would soon reach the old smelt mill, now sadly ruined. We settled down to eat our snack meal. Close by, a pheasant crowed. Matthew said that when the pheasant was first introduced into upper Swaledale, it was known as 'that long-tailed bird', and so attractive did it seem to the dalesfolk, who had been accustomed to looking at birds which were mainly streaky-brown, that some of the pheasants were killed, stuffed and proudly exhibited in local homes.

It was a drought year. We walked to the very head of Swinnergill on the dry bed of what would normally have been a gushing beck. The cliffs closed in on us. We looked ahead through a curtain of rowan leaves and were scolded by a wren. We negotiated the edges of pools and now we heard the boom of water ahead. In periods of heavy rain, the tumbling water and its spray hide one of the celebrated features of Swinnergill—a 70 feet long cave in which, it is claimed, early Nonconformists met for worship at a time of religious intolerance. Others assert that Catholics, of the

Old Faith, gathered there. The story of Swinnergill Kirk is vague in folk memory and unsubstantiated in any texts.

Over the hill lay Crackpot—not to be confused with a place of similar name lying across the valley from Gunnerside. We were looking at a farm that had become a shooting lodge and was now disused, weakened through mining activity. I saw a profusion of spring sandwort, and rails from the mine lying across the top of a wall to discourage sheep from jumping into the next pasture.

Matthew was about nine years old when he was taken to Old Gang, which lies in a valley just off the old route between Low Row and Langthwaite. His guide was Bill Buxton, known to one and all as Annas Bill. In mining-time, men converged on Old Gang from Gunnerside, Low Row, Healaugh and Reeth. Now the big mines were closed, and Annas Bill, Sip and John Tom Rutter worked for themselves, spending their weekdays taking lead ore from the Dam Level. They dressed the ore and heaped up the lead for collection by a cart which took it to Richmond railway station.

Now it was Matthew's turn to show a stranger around Old Gang. We enjoyed the very best of early spring weather. The cock grouse were lively, crowing as they breasted the air, alighting to shout, 'Go-back! Go-back!'

The chimney, Old Gang's most notable surviving feature, is not excessively tall, but well-proportioned, being quite slim and tapering gently with increasing height. A space near the bottom shows its lining of firebricks. The early nineteenth-century smelt mill was three-quarters of the way to becoming a total wreck. A Swaledale 'yow' and its lamb bounded from the cool recesses of an old flue.

We followed the pencil-straight line of the flue as it headed for Healaugh Crag, and then turned to see the remains of the peat house. The steeply pitched gable ends were set 390 feet apart and there were 20 feet between the rows of stone pillars. I heard that enough peat could be stored here to keep the smelt mill operating for a year. The areas from which the peat had come were still to be seen as 'peeat pots', which may have been four or five feet deep but had silted up in recent times.

We walked to Merryfield, about 1,000 feet above sea level, where miners had converted a heather moor into a lunar-type landscape. The course of the Friarfold complex on its way to Arkengarthdale was marked by spoil heaps, hushes and shafts. The 'hushes' were created when watercourses were dammed and the dams released to permit a sudden, scouring torrent to wash away the tops and expose the mineral veins.

Matthew Cherry showed me the subterranean passage known as Brandy Bottle. An incline—or should it be called a decline?—was still fitted with rails on which the old wagons had run. We were impressed by the ingenuity of T'Owd Man, as past generations of miners are collectively known. As in every Dales expedition, there were unexpected moments. A woodcock left the ground not many yards ahead of us. Held between its thighs was one of its young. The old tale about woodcock carrying their offspring was proved true—in this case at least.

Chapter 9

An Artist's Life

Harry Scott loved the company of artists, and from the start the pages of the magazine had a high proportion of drawings. We quite often had an artist on the doorstep, clutching his latest work.

One man arrived with some outstanding oil paintings. Each picture had the horizon exactly half-way down, and the view was over water, looking into the light. This artist, who shall be nameless, would cheerfully ask which bird he should include—once it was a heron, another time tufted duck—and would then depart for a week or two, returning in due course with a superb bird study. He charged for his artwork so much per square inch.

Godfrey Wilson, a former art master at Giggleswick School, regularly appeared at Fellside. This genial man contrived to keep his pipe in his mouth for most of the time. Outdoors he had a jaunty beret on his head and his clothes were a tweedy mixture, scented by woodsmoke. His house at Stainforth was called Kern Knotts, and he had named every room after a mountain or pothole. The lavatory was labelled 'The Long Drop'.

Godfrey was astonishingly versatile. He offered us line drawings in pencil and ink; he provided etchings, and the now unfamiliar process known as drypoint.

When Godfrey had jotted down our requirements, he would return home to his quiet world of the past and draw Dales farmers with collarless shirts, fustian breeches held up by braces and their legs and feet encased in leggings and boots.

Marmaduke Miller also presided over The Falcon at Arncliffe. He had been christened Marmaduke after his father, who was thereafter known as Old Duke, to distinguish him from Young Duke. His mother called him Dick, and to writers he was M'duke! He contributed etchings of Littondale to the earliest issues of the magazine, and in later years had a special fondness for water-colours, dozens of which decked the walls of The Falcon.

As a dalesman born and bred, he really knew the Dales and the transient nature of the climate. He worked mainly in March and April, putting away his art materials in summer when the dale held 1,000 shades of green. 'It's a killing colour,' said the man who liked to use plenty of yellow ochre.

He called Littondale by an older name, Amerdale, and reminded me that Wordsworth, in his *White Doe of Rylstone*, had referred to 'the deep fork of Amerdale'. M'duke enthused about the curlew. I once told him about a Wharfedale farmer's observation that, 'I reckon t'back o' winter's brokken when thou hears a curlew shout.'

Said M'duke, 'That bird is the essence of the dales and moors. It's one of the very few birds that keep you company on a wakeful night. I hear it calling out at all hours. If I was in a foreign country I would not feel homesick—unless I heard a curlew call.'

Fred Lawson, of Castle Bolton in Wensleydale, sent us pictures and a monthly commentary on Dales life. He liked to paint the 'scraggy bits' at the edge of the moors. He wrote very much as he spoke: 'We are having very unpleasant weather. The wind seems to be fixed in the east and, as the old saying goes, "When the wind is in the east it's neither fit for man nor beast." We have either snow showers or very cold rain.' Another month: 'It has been a cold time for the lambs. The first one I saw this year was laid out in front of the stove in the farm kitchen. The next time that I went in, it had got its head up a bit. I remarked on this and was told that it had just had some whisky and warm milk.'

Fred worked out-of-doors in all weathers. I remember

asking him why he had never bought a car, and he told me of artist friends who used a car to go looking for a subject they might paint. They never found anything that satisfied them. 'I set off with my stuff, and after a mile or two I can go no further. I sit down—and paint whatever is to hand.'

Once, as I was preparing an issue for the press, I found that I did not appear to have Fred's drawing or notes. So I rang up the post office in Castle Bolton and asked if a message could be passed to Fred. The woman on the telephone said, 'I thought Fred hadn't posted anything to you this month. He'll be coming in here before long. I'll get him to sit down and write.' She was as good as her word.

'Dear Dalesman,' he wrote. 'The other day it suddenly became spring. All day it was sunny and everything seemed to become green at the same time. After all the cold wet weather it is rather much all at once, and makes you feel somewhat lost . . . I generally go uphill to paint in summer where it's too cold and windswept in winter. The higher up you get, the better the chance of getting away from the vivid green in early summer. About August, either up or down, everything gets more tone. When you get on the moors it doesn't matter what time of the year it is.'

I spent the afternoon of a stormy day with Muriel, Fred's widow, hearing her reminisce about the old days. Fred had moved to Wensleydale when his artist friend George Graham had enthused about it. Another man who was lured from Leeds by favourable reports was Jacob Kramer, but only Fred had remained for any length of time. Muriel, no mean artist herself, told me of the day when Fred had proposed marriage to her.

'One day, Fred was painting the fair at Leyburn. He always loved the colour, movement and excitement of fairgrounds, which were set up in the Dales on the old feast days. I sauntered up the town and there he was, just finishing his picture, putting it down carefully so that nobody would tip it over. He had brought his old briar pipe out of his pocket to have a smoke. He leaned against the Town Hall window sill. I was just 18 years old, but we talked as equals for a minute or two. In the background, a roundabout was operating, the music blaring. Fred just looked at me and said, "Will you marry me?" Just like that. He was absolutely straight.'

Constance Pearson, of Malhamdale, who died in 1970, was a painter of Dales scenery and Dalesfolk who did not wait for the sun to shine before starting work. She was often out and about when cloud drew a curtain of swirling vapour across the sun, and even when her paper was likely to be spattered with rain. She kept water in an old honey jar and her brushes never seemed to hold pure colour.

A painting by this talented artist hangs above my fireplace. A solitary walker is depicted struggling uphill, between banks of snow. He nears a summit cairn. Behind him is an ancient limestone landscape. Penyghent is there and, on the horizon, the Sphinx-like form of Ingleborough. The artist was born and reared in Leeds; she married Sidney Pearson who, though an accomplished painter, lacked the flair revealed by his wife, although his oil paintings were structurally and tonally sound. Constance worked quickly as she captured impressions of the world about her.

She is recalled at Malham as relatively tall, rather quiet, hardy and energetic. She walked for miles in all weathers, showing special powers of endurance in winter, though in her later years she was afflicted with rheumatism. Despite her apparent hardiness, she often had a price to pay for these winter wanderings in the bad throats, chills and back trouble that sometimes followed, though these were soon shrugged off. For the book *Malham and Malham Moor*, which she illustrated in colour, she 'froze' Malham at a rather interesting stage. It was then a real Dales village.

Constance pictured a threshing day during the 1939–45 war, when a powerful Case tractor hauled the thresher up the dale and the farmers had to co-operate fully in delivering the crops to a place beside the Lister's Arms. She painted Malham Fair, a continuation of the old sheep fairs that had formerly been held on the village green. Large collages by Constance Pearson hang above the main staircase at Malham Tarn House. No one portrayed the varied moods of the Dales with more sensitivity and skill.

A sad experience in the early days of *The Dalesman* concerned an oil painting by Reginald Brundrit, RA. The subject was 'The Darkening River' (Wharfe). Brundrit painted on wood—and when it was being returned to him, the wood was shattered. I forget how much compensation he was paid—perhaps £25, a sad blow to a struggling journal.

I never met Brundrit, but the shockwaves of the shattered picture were still detectable when I joined Harry Scott. He lived for many years at Linton, his dwelling a spacious old house, his studio a more modest structure on the hillside above Grassington.

He painted confidently, portraying the landscape and also leaving us some lively studies of dalesfolk, my own favourite being a robust 'Fresh-air Stubbs'.

J. S. Atherton, who died in 1943, was another artist who settled in Wharfedale. He was as much at home with both oil and water-colour mediums as he was with the Dales through which he ceaselessly tramped, looking for subjects. The last Atherton picture I saw was at the home of a man born in Wharfedale and now living—in Iceland. A. Reginald Smith, whose delicate water-colours adorn *The Striding Dales*, a modern classic by Halliwell Sutcliffe, was found drowned at the Strid, where the Wharfe, in the early manhood of its life, is confined to a narrow course by outcropping rock, and the current is dangerously strong.

James Arundel, of Bradford, a wealthy man, not only painted Dales subjects but supplied printing blocks. At that time, a set of blocks might cost from £50 to £80, so it was a considerable temptation to accept them. Once he sent us 'The River Aire at Cottingley', a painting that was somewhat streaky. Soon after publication, a reader submitted her comments in the form of an entertaining couplet:

> Aire River? Nay, nivver—
> But it maks no matter, for I can't see t'watter!

Appropriately, when I first met Joan Hassall, the wood-engraver, the winter sunshine was as intense as a search-light beam; it probed every crack and cranny in the living room of Priory Cottage at Malham. Joan exulted in the brightness and warmth of a day that might have been plucked from summer. A light northerly wind had sharpened the horizons and revealed every feature of the dale with impressive clarity. The detail of the scene was such as you might find on one of her engravings.

One of the most loved English artists, Joan Hassall became well known as a book illustrator. Yet she was never a wealthy person and her life was marked by ill-health and, latterly, by failing eyesight, which caused her to give up engraving in 1977. Her work, though widely appreciated, was not recognised by great honours until, in 1987, the year before her death, she was awarded the OBE. Yet her reputation will endure. She conveyed her own special vision of the world through lines cut on boxwood; she did much to carry on the English tradition of wood engraving that might be said to have begun in the mid-eighteenth century, with the work of Thomas Bewick.

She spent 70 years in London and retired to Malham in 1977, yet she had known the place since 1932 and visited it regularly. I heard from her how she acquired Priory Cottage. It had been bought by Miss Greta Hopkins, an art mistress for whom Joan had a great regard. She asked Joan to help her move in. 'I was sitting in a window seat, looking out, thrilled at everything, when I said, "Isn't it lovely here!" Miss Hopkins said, "Right! I'll leave it to you!"'

I told Joan that I had long admired the work of her writer friend, Margaret Lane, and that the combination of Miss Lane's prose and Joan Hassall's drawings gave a special distinction to what has become a classic book on the Brontës. She told me that they met when Margaret Lane was well advanced with the book. So many pictures were required that Joan had to resort to scraperboard drawings, which could be completed more quickly than engravings. 'We went up to Haworth together. I remember that the boarding accommodation we found was rather small and chilly. There was not really a sitting room, so we used to go to bed very early. Margaret got into bed, and I sat in an old wicker chair, well wrapped up. Then we went through her typescript, deciding what would be good to illustrate.' Margaret Lane had a car, and they would drive about the district, while Joan made sketches. She was fortunate in being loaned some old photographs, so the illustrations for the book were 'a mixture of my sketches and old photographs'.

We looked through some of her albums. 'The entire body of work was formed by just having come to Malham for a holiday. That visit gave me an outlook.' We stood in what Joan called her Work Barn. It was flavoured by apples. A large Albion hand press, made in 1832, was still in perfect working order. She used engraving tools she had purchased in 1931: my first chat with her was in 1981. There was a gentle swish as she applied inker to a wood engraving. She carefully positioned a sheet of paper. The old press thwacked as pressure was applied. Joan peeled from the block of wood a study of a hedgehog. She allowed me to take it away with me.

At her funeral service in Kirkby Malham church, in March, 1988, Brian North Lee said, 'She created a miniature and beguiling world on wood.' It was a gentle, stylish world, with a countryside that predated tractors, transistors and television.

(above) Skipton Castle, for centuries the home of the Cliffords.

(inset) Harry J. Scott, founder of *The Dalesman*.

(below) Clapham, home of *The Dalesman*, in quieter times.

Newby Head, the sheep farm on the old turnpike between Ingleton and Hawes.

A family of 'travellers' en route for the big fair at Appleby.

Austwick, east of Clapham, where the author and his family lived for seven years.

Arnold Brown, guide to Ingleborough Cave, near Clapham.

The rope-maker at Hawes.

A Wensleydale cheese-maker.

Packhorse Bridge, Thorns Gill, Ribblesdale.

The last of the steam road rollers in Settle district negotiates a stretch at Sherwood Brow.

(left) A Dales drystone waller. *(right)* Len Surr, of Keasden, with two sheep on his mooredge smallholding. *(below)* The cellarium at Fountains Abbey near Ripon, where Dales wool was stored.

Horse power in the meadow at Newby Cote, near Clapham.

Haymakers near Clapham sweeping up for pike-making.

Countersett Hall, near Semerwater, contrasting in its
seventeenth-century majesty with the nearby poultry runs.

High Force, Teesdale.

Chapter 10

Limestone Country

Exploring the sweet-and-sour country around Clapham was a continuous delight. Eastwards lay limestone, the largest outcrop in Britain—a pearl-grey landscape, composed of gorges, bare cliffs, 'pavements' and potholes. Westwards from the village was the millstone grit, brownish in hue, swaddled in moist, brown peat, thatched by ling.

The limestone had a major appeal for Harry Scott. He marvelled at its creation 300 million years ago. For him, the limestone lit up the landscape. When he had been a subeditor in Leeds, working at night, trying to sleep by day, any thoughts of the Dales were about living within sight of the pure limestone of the Craven district. On my first visit to Clapham, the stretch of road I remembered best was Buckhaw Brow and the upward sweep of limestone scars to where a kestrel hovered against a powder-blue sky.

Having grown up beside gritstone, I now began to notice some of the special characteristics of limestone—how, for example, there were days when the sky tones were much darker than those of the land; and how the limestone, like the chameleon, might change its hue a hundred times a day according to changes in circumstances, becoming a glorious pink when tinted by sunset rays. Yet for millions of years following its creation, the limestone had been buried deep, overlaid by newer rocks, to appear in the slow process of erosion.

The flowers of the limestone country became my favourites. They stood out clearly from the greys and pale greens of the landscape, and usually demanded little effort if they were to be seen. I scrambled up Penyghent in late March, looking for purple saxifrage, or trudged from Arncliffe to the place where mountain avens grew at its most southerly point in mainland Britain. Years ago, on a certain sheltered hillside, I viewed a plant so rare and beautiful I have not yet recovered from what was a rich emotional experience. I refer to the very rare lady's slipper orchid, with its maroon flowers and distinctive yellow lip.

In my spring jaunts, I located the wet flushes that sustained the bird's eye primrose, beloved of Reginald Farrer, botanist and flower painter, who lived at Clapham. Within viewing distance of my present home at Giggleswick was limestone pavement with grykes (fissures) holding a profusion of plants, many of the woodland type. They kept their heads down and found shade and shelter, as well as sanctuary from the ceaseless grazing of sheep. In spring, the early purple orchis was sharply delineated: the plants stood to attention on the thin soils between the outcropping rock. Later, the ground became spangled by yellow mountain pansies and in shady places the lily of the valley was quite common, its delicate white flowers contrasting with large green leaves. Jacob's Ladder grew beside a limestone cliff. In spring I visited old meadowland on which artificial fertilisers had not been used and glanced appreciatively across damp acres that held the sulphur yellow of globe flowers and the gold of marsh marigold.

I found that limestone terrain had little surface water; that the rain, picking up weak acid in the atmosphere, had slowly dissolved the rock where it had been fractured through 'faulting', creating hundreds of subterranean systems—caves and potholes. If I could have taken a giant knife and cut a slice from mighty Ingleborough, I would have discovered it to be honeycombed.

I watched the peat-stained water thundering into Gaping Gill; I saw the torrent reappear from a cave adjacent to Ingleborough Cave, in Clapdale, and I pondered on the measureless caverns that lay between. When my fascination with caves had risen to fever pitch, I met two remarkable men—Tot Lord and Norman Thornber.

Tot, who lived at Settle, was a greengrocer who had little appetite for shop-work or, indeed, for work of any nature unless it related to his primary interest: archaeology. He was an amateur in his field who knew how to pick the brains of men like Arthur Keith and Boyd Dawkins. They in turn were fascinated by this dalesman's breezy manner. E. H. Partridge, the scholarly headmaster of Giggleswick School, would meet him by the Ribble Deeps, sharing Tot's interest in wildfowl and angling. Partridge noted that the brightness of Tot's face was distinctive—'a red face which in the fading light had the dull glow of old baked brick.'

Tot presided over the Pig Yard Club, the name being taken from a small building in the yard owned by Tot's family. It became a 'cal 'oil', or place of conversation. Much of the talk was about local cave archaeology.

The most famous 'bone cave' in the district, Victoria Cave, had been extensively excavated and its mouth was now a yawning hole on the scars. Yet in 1925, the members of the Pig Yard Club found a stalagmite floor in the extension of the cave and from beneath the floor came the remains of Ice Age mammals, situated in part of a bone layer described by Richard Tidelman in the 1870s. He had been able to show that this deposit was older than the last glacial period. Tot's finds included the remains of hippopotamus, narrow-nosed rhinoceros, straight-tusked elephant, giant deer, spotted hyena and brown bear. They had roamed the Dales during a period when the climate was warm, about 120,000 years ago.

In 1935, Sir Arthur Keith—having attended a meeting of the British Association in Norwich—set out with a friend for 'the caves and moors of Yorkshire'. He related in his autobiography that, on reaching Settle, he inquired about Tot, who had sent him bones for examination, but being unable to discover where he was, set off up the steep road which leads to the high moorland plateau lying immediately to the east of Settle.

Sir Arthur and his companion were looking for Victoria Cave, which had been so well described by Boyd Dawkins in his book *Cave Hunting*. As they drove along, they became aware of a somewhat untidy van being driven at speed behind them. Sitting on top of the van, urging the driver to greater efforts and briskly waving his arms to attract attention, was a young man whom Sir Arthur later discovered to be Tot Lord. Frustrated at having missed the great man during his visit to Settle, Tot had set off in noisy pursuit.

In 1937 the Pig Yard Club museum was moved to the former Primitive Methodist Chapel, and this building became known as Wapping Hall. There was virtually everything behind glass, even a stuffed badger. On the wall was the coat of arms of the Club, with its pig's head, rope ladder, pick and spade, dragonesque brooch and a human bone with gladiatorial sword. One of the most unusual sights at Settle in the 1930s was that of Lady Boyd Dawkins helping in the hayfield. Thomas Lord, snr, rented land and farmed on a modest scale. The Boyd Dawkins' wanted Tot to take them onto the hills and he could not do this until a 'straight edge' had been secured in the hayfield—hence her ladyship's offer of help.

Tot Lord was an individualist. Who but Tot would have taken (on a week-long excavation of a site on Malham Moor) a marquee and a bed with a brass head? Who but Tot would have installed a stove in the rock shelter known as Sewell's Cave? When he was working there on a Sunday, his wife arrived with the ingredients of a good lunch. It was cooked to a turn and served complete with Yorkshire pudding.

Tot's later days were spent at Town Head, a large Victorian house with spacious grounds. To walk up the drive to the house from the top of Constitution Hill was to enter a world that, with its dense shrubbery, its old palm tree and the house with its glass-and-iron verandah, might almost have been part of a film set for a story penned by Somerset

Maugham. Butterflies by the score occupied the sunlit days in visiting the many buddleias. Beneath the verandah reposed a wicker chair, a table—and the skull of an elephant!

If Tot was not otherwise engaged, he would cordially invite the visitor to see his museum. This occupied a large ground floor room. I would watch the ritual of unlocking the door, and then I had a glorious insight into prehistoric life through the many exhibits. Here lay the skull of a great cave bear, and over there was a reverse-barbed harpoon fashioned from antler. Dragonesque brooches had a case to themselves. Tot was a great maker of cases; he was security minded. I remember him producing what he called 'the bone of contention', an object from Victoria Cave with doubtful origins. Was it from a human being or a wild animal?

When I visited the museum 'on spec' with J. B. Priestley, Tot was quick to open it up. During the tour, I said to a local man, 'To really understand these objects, we should try to get into the mind of Early Man.' JB had been listening. He retorted, 'The great thing for civilisation today is to get out of the mind of Early Man.' Tot Lord died in October, 1965.

* * *

Norman Thornber, bachelor, followed in the corn merchant's business started by his father, W. W. Thornber, who lived fully to an immense age. I recall him driving his car, and smoking a cigar, when he was over 90. One of the best-kept secrets of *The Dalesman* was the authorship of the diary of a Dales farmer—a popular feature of the magazine for years. So that he might express his opinions forcefully, as a Dales farmer would do, Norman asked that his name should not be associated with it, and as far as I know this is the first time the two have been linked.

It was Norman's enthusiasm for limestone, and more precisely for potholing, that led me to a (mercifully short) career as a potholer. He was one of the first wardens of the Cave Rescue Organisation and the author of a most successful book which *Dalesman* published and which listed all known cave systems, with details of their features and accurate measurements. The CRO came a close second to his religion—he was a devout Catholic—and he spoke about it incessantly.

I have already mentioned my sense of wonderment at seeing Fell Beck tumble into the main shaft of Gaping Gill, on Ingleborough. Norman encouraged me to visit Gaping Gill when the Bradford Pothole Club had installed a winch and bosun's chair for the 340 foot descent. (No charge was made for the descent, but the Club requested 10s for hauling a visitor back up!) Norman decided that he would stay on the surface; I was strapped into the bosun's chair, which hung from light scaffolding. When a plank was removed, I dangled above the void from which rose fine vapour, most of the beck having been diverted, as was the custom, so that there would be no obligatory shower. The brake was eased from the drum of the winch, which began to revolve under my weight. The damp, mossy walls of the upper shaft went by slowly, becoming a blur when we were clear of the sides. The technicoloured world of the fellside was replaced by a range of greys as I found myself looking into the cathedral-sized main chamber. One visitor has compared himself to a spider dangling from inside the dome at St Paul's.

The chair slid smoothly beside the cable which guided it to a dryish part of the floor. I heard a hissing sound as a fine spray of water struck the perpetually damp pebbles on the floor of a cavern as large as a football pitch. The voices of potholers reached me with a strange echoing effect. Far below, I could see them moving about the chamber, their headlamps burning. It was rather like seeing a group of fireflies—only each light was at the other end!

The descent took some 20 seconds, and the headlong dash into the underworld slowed a little as the ground approached. The effect, as I looked up, was of a ruined cathedral, its strong vertical lines curving in with height to where daylight, the colour filtered out by spray, appeared from a rent in the roof.

Eli Simpson, of Settle, a caving enthusiast whose speciality was keeping records, allowed me to photograph an artist's impression of the first descent of Gaping Gill in Victorian days by the Frenchman Martel. It showed a bearded man on a ladder made of rope. Eli told me of his efforts to photograph the grandeur of the main chamber with his trusty plate camera, the plates having 'slow' emulsions. He set up the camera, and then distributed about the chamber heaps of flashpowder resting on newspaper. The lens of the camera was left open and, one by one, the heaps of flashpowder were ignited, each heap offering a brilliant display of light—and much smoke. Eventually, the chamber was so smoky he had a problem locating the camera. He advised other photographers to do this by paying out a ball of string and winding it up when the work was done.

Another day, Norman arranged a trip to Bruntscar Cave, behind the farmhouse of that name in Chapel-le-Dale. It was an old 'show' cave, he said, the implication being that all one need do was walk in. In the event, it soon became a crawling job. Norman had some stomach trouble that day, so he could not accompany Brian and myself as we explored. We moved into a small chamber, which was receiving a torrent of water. We must progress further by breasting the water and climbing into a stream passage.

Once in the passage, my body took on the shape of a question mark because of protruding formations and the necessity to advance in a curiously bent position. The passage was narrow and, at the time we used it to reach the heart of Whernside, was a quarter full of racing, foam-flecked water that appeared to be rising even as we looked at it. Prudence decreed that we return. I recall arriving at the point where the water, now a ferocious torrent, spilled into the little chamber. I sat down in the stream, this being the only way to drop safely into the chamber. For a second or two I was conscious of damming up the beck. The water was rising up my back! I leapt, landed with tons of water around me and followed Brian to the daylight, where Norman was feeling a little better than he had been.

His great work, *Pennine Underground*, is a lasting memorial to a meticulous man on whom potholers might rely. They called the book their 'bible', and were pleased that the maps showed the underground systems in relation to the wall pattern, a most sensible idea. Norman himself did not long outlive his father.

* * *

There came to *The Dalesman* a young Lancashire journalist, Ian Plant, who soon became fascinated by the 1,000 underground systems of the Craven limestone. I recall that when his interest was developing fast, an outbreak of foot-and-mouth disease occurred. Visitors to the Craven district were asked not to leave the roads for fear of picking up and spreading infection by the simple process of walking about. There was one way in which I could help Ian renew his acquaintance with the caves—and that was to ask Mabel Sharpe, of White Scar Cave, if he could venture a little beyond the public section of this 'show' system. She agreed, for I had been 'letting in the New Year' at White Scar, and thus comforting her strongly superstitious mind. (When she had first asked me, I was the 'dark-haired stranger' of folklore, but as the years went by the hair thinned and became a little wintry in appearance. Nonetheless, she expected me to turn up at noon on January 1, and no one was allowed to enter the cave until I had visited the pay box and a good deal of the main passage. I then had coffee and Christmas cake in her bungalow before returning to less fanciful activities.)

Ian collected his potholing clothes; he changed into them at the end of the show-cave, then did a belly-flop into the subterranean stream, hitting the water with a resounding 'thwack' and surfacing with a broad smile on his face. With Ian and others I explored some of the major systems, the last for me being Alum Pot, above Selside. I had no difficulty in following the cave system to the open shaft, in negotiating the bridge and reaching the sump. But on the 60 foot pitch, the start of the return journey, I suffered the indignity of being double-lifelined and virtually hauled up. I concluded that potholing was not for someone of my build.

Ian moved from *The Dalesman* to the *Craven Herald*, which he edited with distinction. His interest in potholing continued with unabated enthusiasm and he used special breathing equipment to explore underground systems. He died in a flooded passage. The huge attendance at his funeral testified to his charm and popularity.

Chapter 11

Men of Wensleydale

Kit Calvert, of Hawes, was The Compleat Dalesman—
somewhat larger than life and ultra-conscious of his Dales
roots and surroundings. I first met Kit in 1953, when he was
already a considerable character. He was leaning against a
parapet of Hawes Bridge, holding his little terrier and
smoking a clay pipe. He removed a battered trilby and
dropped it on the road, where it remained until our meeting
was over.

I last met him on a golden afternoon, beside the high road
from Askrigg into Swaledale, as the BBC filmed another
Herriot series. Kit had brought along Dolly, his pony, a
lively veteran of 18 years. While she took part in a film
sequence, we chatted about this and that. Kit rammed some
strong tobacco into his pipe. It was now a briar, clay pipes
being too hard to come by.

When he had puffed away for a few seconds, and
clouded the air with smoke that made the eyes of passing
crows water, he nodded towards one of the 'extras', who
had been dressed up to represent an old dalesman. 'See yon
chap?' said Kit, with verbal economy. I nodded. 'He came
up to me and said, "Am I talkin' right?" He wasn't really,
but what can you say to a chap whose nivver bin to t'Dales
afore?'

Kit was reared at Burtersett. He went into farming, first
as a farm man and then on his own account, in the grim
days after the 1914–18 war. In the 1930s he became the
saviour of the cheese factory at Hawes, when there was a
strong likelihood that it would close down. He revived the

business, after many an anxious moment, in 1935, when it had a working capital of £1,085. Thirty-one years later, it was sold for almost half a million pounds, and Kit was free to please himself, which meant upgrading his leisure-time interests, with some Preaching of the Word, some book-selling, much reading, and many a 'crack' with his cronies.

He was an avid reader. At the age of nine, he had howled at his father and demanded, of all things, a Collins clear-type dictionary, price one shilling. His howling brought results, although his father was a poor quarryman. About 1927, Kit started collecting books, his idea being to build up a library of Yorkshire publications, but—said he—'it's developed over the fells to Cumberland and Westmorland since then.'

One of the rooms of his house was almost furnished with books—well over 2,000 of them. 'I keep missen poor with this job,' he told me. 'They are going to find some rubbish when I've gone.' He showed me a copy of Ogilby's *Book of Roads* (1698) which he had bought at a farm sale in Swaledale about five years before. 'I'd to buy over six hundredweight of books to get this . . . I didn't bother to bring the others away!'

Born at Burtersett in 1903, Kit grew up in the most humble of circumstances but with determination and an appetite for work. He walked a round trip of three miles to school at Hawes. His mid-day meal, packed up by mother, was two slices of buttered bread, with a filling of jam, marmalade or treacle. He had a regular job at the age of ten, and he left school a few weeks before his thirteenth birth-day. There followed a round of farm work that gravely taxed the energies of a 'lile lad'. His employer was a lead miner who had retired from the underworld with a hacking cough—the old 'gruver's complaint'—and could do little work himself. Eventually, when Kit's pleas for extra 'brass' went unheeded, he attended the 'hirings', and was as-tonished to be hired at the magnificent sum of £1 a week —with board included.

Five years later, when he was injured, he had to leave

and take light work. His spirit and wits were unimpaired: he regrouped his meagre resources, went into raising livestock on his own account, suffered the trauma of the Depression and, as it was beginning to ease, took up the cause of local farmers who had fallen on hard times with the collapse of Hawes creamery.

Though he was insolvent himself, with just a few domesticated animals as assets, Kit struggled on, looking for financial support for a revived enterprise. He triumphed in the end and, becoming the company secretary of Wensleydale Dairy Products, Ltd., he agreed to work for a year without pay; his scale of remuneration could be decided when the first balance sheet was produced!

This is the gist of what I heard during dozens of conversations. His wife died—or, as Kit would have said, she was 'called home'—in 1975. They had been married for 44 years.

When I visited him we would look at books or survey the well-equipped playing area in the croft outside, that Kit provided for any bairn who wished to use it. He was extremely fond of Dales pictures, especially one by Janet Rawlins—a study of a Dales window, decorated for Christmas, with a view outwards of a snowy world. The painting had been commissioned for a Christmas issue of *The Dalesman*.

Kit's religion was an integral part of the man and not something to be demonstrated on Sunday. He was one of the old-style Congregationalists—a chapel man—fervent in his preaching and praying, with homely illustrations and many a good dialect word or expression to add savour and local interest. He needed little encouragement to read from his translations of passages from the Bible. 'Some folk say I shouldn't have translated the Good Book into Yorkshire Dales dialect. I tell 'em 'at our Lord spoke in dialect, and that usually quietens 'em . . .'

In December, I would persuade him to read from his version of the Christmas story. He would pick up the modest publication that had been run off on a friend's duplicator, and announce, with solemnity, 'St Luke's Gospel. Chapter Two.' And off he went. I had a special love for the dialect-speaking Angel: 'Dooan't bi freetened, fer ther's nowt t' bi freetened on, for Ah's fetchen ye good news ev gert joy fer aw t'world. Fer ther's bin booarn t'day i' David's toon, a Saviour, Christ the Lord. An' ta prove t'ye 'at it is seea, ye'll finnd t'babby lapped i' a barrie cooat an' liggen in a manger.'

Picture the Prodigal returning to his father after a dissolute phase of his life. When his father has shown his joy at the reunion, the lad says: 'Fatther, Ah've sinned agen heaven an' dun a gert wrang t'ye, an' Ah's nut fit t' bi coa'd a lad ev yours.' Or picture Jesus walking by the lake—'tarn' in Dales parlance—and seeing the disciples fishing. 'He ca'ed oot tew 'em, "Lads, hey ye caught owt?" Th' shooted back, "Nowt!" Sooa He sez, "Kest yert net ower t'reet side 'ev t'booat an' ye'll git a catch."' Which, of course, they did.

Kit's surplus books found a temporary home in a single-roomed shop he rented. The many shulves were packed with books, mainly Victorian religious works or fading copies of long-published romances, each story guaranteed to have the sun setting on the young couple in the last paragraph. With so many yellowing pages, and a damp atmosphere, Kit's bookshop had a musty flavour. Here, in the early days, I would see his old friend, John Mason, an ex-railwayman whose love of books matched that of Kit but who concentrated on mental improvement to the extent of studying the classics. He had a notice in the bookshop window: 'Hawes University. Bursar—John Mason.'

When no one was in attendance, Kit trustingly left the door of the bookshop unlocked. If anyone wished to buy a book, they could leave the money in a circular wooden tray, of the type used for collections in a Nonconformist chapel.

Towards the end of 1983, he invited me to Hawes and then produced from a drawer an article he had written for *The Dalesman*, which he had taken since its earliest days. Kit's article was no academic piece for which a lot of research had been needed, but something that was within his experience—the importance of gezlings, or goslings, to the quarrymen's families and others in the Hawes district up to the time of the 1914–18 war.

The breadwinner's wage at the quarry was between 16s and 18s a week, and every penny was needed. The food required to feed the family, and for other necessities, had to be obtained 'on strap', by credit, to be paid for when the goslings were sold. The local grocer and draper would give limited credit when a wife or mother of a quarryman said, 'Ye'll hev t'give us a bit o' time until we've seld gezlings. But we'll pay ye ivvery hawpenny.'

Kit read out his article, including the story of his Aunt Lizzie, whose favourite old goose nested under the kitchen table. She laid her eggs and sat on them for a month before the goslings were hatched. You had to put a board in front of the nest before sitting at the table to a meal. 'Anyone who failed to do this got a nasty nip from the goose.'

Back in the office, I had Kit's article typeset and in due course he was sent a proof. Meanwhile, I had found a photograph of him complete with clay pipe, and a drawing by Janet Rawlins of the geese at Gayle. Kit returned the proof with a brief note that he was 'off colour' but would be much better when the spring weather came. A few days later, his death was announced. He was 80 years old. His dying wish was honoured when, on the day of the funeral, his pony Dolly hauled a cart on which the coffin reposed.

* * *

A dalesman of a different type was Dick Chapman, born and reared at Askrigg but, during his later life, domiciled at Bainbridge, in a cottage just a few yards from the Bain, the shortest river in England. The presence of the Bain was important to Dick: he enjoyed 'crabbing', which is the Dales term for catching crayfish, the freshwater lobsters.

The son of a butcher, Dick had a good education and became a schoolteacher, spending most of his career at Shipley and Bingley. In 1927 he began camping holidays for his schoolboys in Wensleydale. He was fascinated by prehistory and thrilled when, in 1938, while conducting a party of town lads along the shore of Bainbridge, one of them picked up a Bronze Age spearhead. It was his most treasured possession. He sometimes showed it to me and yarned about Semerwater and the story of a city flooded because of its inhospitality—a story given stylish poetic treatment by William Watson.

I gathered from Dick that the *Ballad of Semerwater* is a richly embroidered account of a story that has come down through local folk memory from the remote past, being Christianised in the process to become yet another medieval morality tale. When, in 1937, the level of Semerwater fell over two feet following the dredging of its outflow, the Bain, there came to light objects associated with Bronze and Iron Age folk who had settled in this sheltered pocket in the hills above Wensleydale. Close to the shore, on what had apparently been an artificial island, were found traces of wooden piles. Pieces of bone and flint were collected.

The famous spearhead, found plastered by clay, was nonetheless easily spotted. Dick Chapman felt that the occupants of this lakeside settlement must have gone in a hurry. The man who left the valuable spearhead clearly did so at a time of panic; it would, said Dick, be like a modern man deserting a Rolls Royce. Semerwater is notorious for its flash floods. Was the lakeside settlement overwhelmed by a nocturnal torrent of water following a cloudburst on the fells?

I heard from Dick how in recent times a party of campers hurriedly retreated at night when water entered the tents they had pitched by Semerwater. And the occupants of a caravan, sensing something unusual had taken place, stepped from their bunks at night—into several inches of water.

Dick first knew Semerwater as a small child in 1900. He had a fund of entertaining stories, which he told to callers at his Bainbridge cottage or to the occupants of the bar at the Rose and Crown across the way. In 1900, he was one of a group taken to the district in horse-drawn vehicles, traps and wagonettes. They did not go the whole way: the journey to Semerwater was completed on foot. As the party returned the members followed a footpath which led through a farmhouse that had been constructed across an old right of way. The occupants of the house showed no surprise when complete strangers crossed the room in which they were having a meal!

Another time, Dick and a cousin decided to swim across Semerwater from the inflow to the Carlow Stone, a huge block of ice-borne stone near the outflow of the lake. When the two lads were over half-way, they noticed horse-drawn vehicles arriving. The Pentecostal League was holding a service, and soon a hymn was being sung. It was vital for the swimmers to recuperate before attempting to return to where they had left their clothes, so they rested neck-deep in the water. On their return, they found that cows had nuzzled their clothes. One cow began to chew a shirt, and Dick's cousin shouted, 'Put that ruddy shirt down!' He had not reckoned with the fine acoustics of Semerwater at lake level. The lads were told later that one of the religious party at the Carlow Stone had begun to speak about St Paul, and was quoting one of Paul's utterances when the distraught call about the shirt was heard.

Dick Chapman was my main informant about crayfish. For years, he knew where all the local otters were to be found by the remains of crayfish on the flat stones the animals frequented during the night. Fishing for crayfish was taken so seriously in Wensleydale that special rules were introduced to govern it. They no longer apply.

The equipment needed for the sport was a stick to which was attached about four feet of string, a stone on the string acting as a weight. A hand-net must be at hand. The bait used for crayfish was frequently a piece of liver, but Dick Chapman preferred pieces of intestine from cow or sheep. An experienced crabber would go to where there was a flattish stone over which the water flowed gently, knowing that in such conditions the scent of the bait would be well distributed. 'Crayfish might be seen crawling from under the stones and moving towards the bait,' said Dick. 'They are quarrelsome things. I watched two meet. They forgot the food and had a fight instead.' Patience and a steady hand were needed when removing the bait and the crayfish from the water. Try hurrying the process and the crayfish became suspicious.

Crayfish were caught in late summer. Dick Chapman recalled when the Vyners of Studley had the grouse-shooting on Askrigg Moor. After dinner on the Twelfth, they processed to the river between Yore Bridge and Worton Bridge to 'crab'. The river had already been baited by members of their staff: the visitors merely removed the baited lines and coaxed the crayfish into the nets, from which they were transferred into buckets. The best of the catch was eaten at dinner on the following day. Local lads simply walked down to the river with their home-made tackle. Dick Chapman and his friends could catch 200 crayfish in one expedition. The boys sometimes tested each other's courage by allowing crayfish to nip their fingers, progressing from quite small fish to the big ones. 'I have been nipped almost down to the bone,' Dick told me. 'When a really big crayfish took hold, you could not easily remove it. In the end, you had to lay the crayfish on the ground—and stamp on it!'

In Dick's day, crayfish were cooked by being dropped into a pan of boiling water, where they turned a brilliant red. A large pan would hold from 50 to 60 fish, which were cooked for half-an-hour, when the flesh was revealed as firm and white. The tail of a crayfish was considered the supreme delicacy. During the 1939–45 war, Dick had a salad with crayfish on top and hard-boiled eggs from a gullery set round about.

Old folk in Wensleydale recalled the activities of one Sproates Blades, an outstanding angler in the Ure, who was commissioned to provide 1,000 live crayfish for the stocking of a Scottish reservoir. Sproates and a friend obtained the required number in just under two hours. The crayfish were kept alive overnight in bags sunk in Gayle Beck. Next morning, they were lifted into milk kits and taken to Scotland by train. No losses of crayfish were reported.

Dick Chapman died in August, 1981, aged 86. We printed in *The Dalesman* tributes from Marie Hartley, Joan Ingilby and David Hall. From David came the story—told to him by Dick—of an Askrigg family ground down by poverty and forced to leave the village. As they made their way down the main street, with a horse and a cart containing all they possessed, at four o'clock in the morning, all their neighbours turned out and sang, 'God be with you till we meet again.' Later, a son returned to pay the family's debts —including one owing to the butcher, Dick's father.

Chapter 12

Close to Nature

In early spring, curlews were in song flight above the meadows on the edge of Clapham: the sound of their trilling reached us loud and clear as we worked on *The Dalesman*. The first of the returning curlews were often to be heard when there was mist, which signified a thaw. One night I heard parties of them passing over, uttering their contact calls. Next morning, as I waited for the bus, with a parcel for our Bentham office, I saw a bird perched on the capstone of a wall, distinguished by its lanky form, its streaky-brown plumage and the scimitar-shaped bill.

In the headlong rush of spring, I would watch a curlew climb steeply on its powerful wings, to hang in the air, a feathered kite. Then, with body angled forwards, it would begin its shallow song glide and a rich, bubbling trill would sound far and wide.

The curlew was the first bird I photographed from a hide. I had made this structure of metal rods and hessian when the gamekeeper told me of a woodcock nest. The gamekeeper's man helped me carry it to one of the high woods near Clapham. He said, 'Prop it against yon wall,' and he took me to within a few feet of where a woodcock sat on the woodland floor amid the russet leaves against which the bird blended perfectly. When taking a photograph with a long lens, I saw my inverted reflection in its eye.

I returned early on the following day. The woodcock rose from the nest and beat its wings slowly, in agitation. On the ground were new-hatched chicks. I did not intrude on their quiet world again.

The curlew would not permit such liberties. A local farmer allowed me to put up the hide on a nest in his meadow, within sight of the village. I moved the hide nearer on successive days. A friend saw me into the hide for photography and soon I had the thrill of seeing a thoroughly wild bird stalking to within a few yards of where I sat. The curlew stood above the eggs, rearranged them and settled down to brood. In the heat of the sunny afternoon, the bird's bill was open and it panted continuously.

The curlew became uneasy and sank lower and lower until it looked as inconspicuous as a clod of dry vegetation. The beak was so low it was hidden by the tufts of grass; from my hide I saw only the hump of the mottled body, the rounded head and a big, bright eye. Long after the curlew had first shown distress, I heard the drone of a light aircraft. What do the curlew's descendants think about the low-flying jets that torment us all today?

The wheezy cry and tumbling flight of the lapwing are distinctive features of the Dales spring. Patches of ill-drained land were called 'tewit grund', and farm lads earned pocket money collecting 'tewit' eggs for sale. Now this is illegal. In any case, widespread improvement to the landscape, with drainage and planting of fields with commercial strains of grass, have reduced the bird's ranks. The only lapwing I photographed at its nest was a splendid male, as the extremely long headcrest testified. The photographs were taken in late May, which in itself was astonishing. I had conducted a service at a remote Bowland chapel when I was told of this dilatory pair. I returned with hide and camera to obtain some pictures.

For me, no day spent tramping across the northern fells is complete without a glimpse of a raven. In the days when Bill Robson and I haunted the Pennines, we had an early spring excursion to a deep gorge where the raven, a bird sacred to the Norsemen, began its nesting activity as early as January, with the collection of large twigs to provide its nest with sure foundations.

Mist lay across the northern Pennines like a damp, grey

shroud. It swirled around the gorge where 50 foot high cliffs stood deep in a litter of boulders, clods of earth and displaced rowan trees. Bill was much at home in such a setting. We followed a sheep trod beside the beck, listening to the clear piping of a cock ring ouzel. Of course, Bill found the nest—on a ledge of rock near the water. We heard the 'zit, zit' of a dipper retreating fast and low.

Then we heard the gruff 'pruk' of a raven in flight. The ring ouzel resumed its piping. Stones clattered as two sheep ran from a patch of succulent grass close to the water and took an upward path. They moved with the verve of mountain goats. High up the gorge, in an almost sterile landscape of cliffs and screes, the mist thinned and at last the raven was glimpsed—a bird played hide-and-seek with us, using the mist for cover.

The nest we sought was an untidy heap of dead twigs on a ledge 30 feet above the stream. Twigs added most recently were from thorn and rowan, but in the older, lower deposits were pieces of gorse and heather stalks. Bill told me of a pair of ravens possibly even this pair—that built a nest on a ledge that was snow-covered. Consequently, when the thaw came the nest tumbled into the gorge. We found a firm nest and a solitary nestling lying on a mattress composed of sheep wool. The nestling was well fed, having had the undivided attention of its parents. I scrambled to a ledge near the nest. The young raven called, the sound being a crow-like 'karr'. Maybe it was feeling irritable. A piece of hair had become lodged under the lid of one eye, which had lost its sparkle. I picked up the raven, waited for its first struggles of indignation to end and drew out the hair. The eye soon began to regain its brightness.

A close relative, the carrion crow, is big, bold and highly intelligent. It struts around the Dales country with a suit as black as that of an undertaker, with beady eyes that miss nothing and a stubble of thick hairs around the base of its beak as though it had not shaved for weeks. It can make a farmer or gamekeeper weep through its depredations, but even the crow's life has a touching domestic aspect, as John

Robinson and I found when we located a nest in a typical position—an isolated rowan—on an otherwise desolate Giggleswick Common.

Sheep bones and coarse wood had been worked into this nest, which was lagged with wool. Crows that have not been much disturbed allow a close approach before they panic and fly off. At this nest, the brooding bird was slow to move. Perhaps it was because it had to run a gauntlet of angry curlews, which dived steeply on it with yelps and the whoosh of displaced air as they applied their air brakes.

The young crows were repulsive creatures, naked except for wisps of hair. Their long necks seemed to have the consistency of India rubber. When a movement near the nest alerted the young birds to a possibility of food, the necks straightened instantly. For a time the nestlings were all mouth and stomach and the days passed with long periods of sleep and short, lively spells of being fed. Soon, with feathers sprouting and appetites quickening, the two surviving crows resembled quickly-flowering tulips. As I reached the nest, up went their heads, and their beaks parted to reveal bright red gapes. The inevitable happened. A farmer discovered the nest and the surviving young were destroyed.

In Stockdale, above Settle, so few trees are to be found that one pair of crows built on a wall-top, the nest sprawling across a couple of capstones. Sheep bones were worked into the coarse structure. Then news reached me from a farm towards Airton that a pair had built their nest—on the ground. This most unusual nest was a depression, lined with wool. A crow rose from the nest at my approach, and the eggs were indeed those of crows rather than of some other ground-nesting species. Alas, when I was excitedly anticipating the eggs hatching, an excessively wet spell arrived and the sodden nest was deserted. Presumably this pair of crows returned to the custom of nesting in trees!

*　　　*　　　*

I went 'birding' with Stan Lythe of Grassington. He had
spent most of his life in Leeds, where he served in the Fire
Service. In retirement at Grassington, he had a less exacting
job with a local builder and had time to explore the neigh-
bourhood. Soon he had responded to the lure of bird
photography. By this time, permission to photograph birds
at their nests was needed from the Nature Conservancy.
Stan complied. Soon he was photographing kingfishers at
Winterburn and oystercatchers on the gravel beds of the
Skirfare, in Littondale. He took his equipment to Grassington Moor for ring ouzel and golden plover. He began to visit
Scotland. A Methodist minister at Grassington put him in
touch with friends in East Anglia, where the stone curlew
awaited his attention. Perhaps the highlight of his career as
a photographer was when he focused his camera on one of
the most rare and charismatic of British birds—a dotterel.
That moment when he lay within a foot or so of the nest of
this mountain-top species was the culmination of years of
effort. Each winter, he had 'genned up' about dotterels,
images of the bird coloured his dreaming. In spring, as we
tramped on the high Pennines, we sometimes saw a 'trip' of
these confiding birds. Stan's camera-finger twitched at the
thought of what he might do, given good fortune on a
Scottish ben.

Kath, his wife, cheerfully tolerated his obsession with
dotterels. There came a time, however, when Stan felt with
her that enough was enough. He planned his last great
expedition. After some frustration, he was climbing from a
glen to the edge of a dotterel-moor when a bird came into
view. That day he found the sitting member of the pair. The
nest lay within a few yards of a path frequented by walkers.
Stan and Kath had to delay photography until all was quiet.
He obtained his photographs and returned to Yorkshire.

I recall a certain Sunday evening—a sunny evening
—when my wife and I, walking through Settle, heard the
squealing of a car's brakes. The car that stopped abruptly
was left parked at a curious angle in relation to the kerb. A
radiant Stan came dashing towards us. We did not need to

be told his special news about dotterels. Then it was back to other species, including the greenshank, spirit of the lonely floe country of Sutherland . . .

In the Dales, Stan became interested in black grouse. He found a lekking ground in the autumn, which was no mean feat. The traditional tourney ground of the blackcock comes alive at the dawning of the day in spring, when these blue-black males face up to each other, pair by pair; they puff out their wattles, droop their wings, coo like pigeons and hiss with an explosive sound, like air rushing out of a cycle valve. It is all part of the ritual of securing the best ground and thus the special attention of any females, the greyhens, that arrive for mating.

With photography in mind, Stan studied the afternoon display and realised that it was not as fervent as the dawn performance but that it provided photographic possibilities, at least until the end of April. With his usual generosity, he offered me the use of the hide. It was on the moors near Malham. What time should I arrive there? 'Ten to four,' he told me. I went at 2-30—and had a long wait. Small 'windows' in the sides of the hide offered a view over white-ground (*Nardus stricta*). In contrast, the lek resembled coconut matting, having been well trodden by the displaying birds.

A blackcock is, in the words of a Dales gamekeeper, 'as big as a littlish turkey!' It cannot be overlooked. I do not claim that the first of the blackcocks arrived at 'ten to four', but as I quietly dozed in the late afternoon, I was aware of excitement on the lekking ground. Birds arrived individually, from several directions. Within minutes, the assembly was complete, with half a dozen pairs. Strange sounds, cooings and hissings, like echoes from prehistory, made the moorland air shiver. I viewed the outer world through the long lens of my camera, which the nearest cock birds seemed too busy to notice. Stan appeared to have placed his hide on an important part of the lek. I heard a rustling sound and realised that a blackcock was pushing its way between a guy rope and the hessian! In due course, the

excitement abated. The birds departed, but would return—
bright and shining—at first light.

Stan, using a fireman's skill and wiles, made a tree hide
with a metal base so that he could photograph herons.
When he climbed the tree it swayed alarmingly, and I was
glad he did not invite me to join him. I have mentioned his
photography of kingfishers. Ingeniously, he used the car as
a hide.

Then he reported he had set up a pylon hide beside the
nest of a pair of green woodpeckers. He did all the work,
watching the birds, finding the hole in the tree, building a
(somewhat shaky) structure and placing the usual hessian-
covered hide within a reasonable distance of that hole. His
activity had taken place in one of the ancient tracts of
woodland overlooking Langstrothdale and the squat tower
of the little church at Hubberholme.

On the evening I photographed the woodpeckers, I met
Stan at his home in Grassington. As we motored up the
dale, he smiled and remarked, 'I hope one of the woodpeckers doesn't attack the pylon. It's made of wood I took
from an old cottage we're renovating—and it's full of
woodworm!'

It was a golden evening. On the previous day, Stan had
had to cope with indifferent conditions. He told me that the
woodpeckers had young and were visiting them with food
at hourly intervals. He saw me into the hide, then departed
for an hour-and-a-half. The vigil was pleasant. Evening
sunlight banded the wood with yellow. I heard the ceaseless refrain of a willow warbler, then the yaffle of a green
woodpecker, some way off . . .

My eye, pressed against the camera's viewer, took in the
area of the nest. The sun was low enough for its rays to
reach the tree at a helpful angle: that hole was illuminated
as though with a spotlight. A sudden flash of bright colours
—green, yellow, red—resolved itself into a woodpecker.
As it clung to the bark, just below the hole, the bird might
have been a Dales parrot. The chirring of the young stimulated it to clamber quickly to the nesting hole. The wood-

pecker fed them rapidly, then it was away. I thought my
camera had jammed. In fact, I had exposed an entire film!
Stan told me that at one feed, the young birds craned out so
far that one fell to the ground. Stan slipped it in an anorak
pocket, shinned up the tree and replaced the helpless bird
in the hole.

When Stan died, he had been planning to go to Scotland
again—to photograph golden eagles!

*   *   *

Derek Bunn introduced me to the daily lives of barn owls in
the wild west of Yorkshire. From a hide of wood and
hessian, set against a dark green bank of spruce, I watched
the owls going about their business. There were evenings
of brilliant sunlight and evenings when the rain fell with a
tropical intensity. I settled in the hide with binoculars,
coffee in a flask and midge cream in a handy dispenser. On
the warmest, stillest evenings the midges danced in the air
like wreaths of brown smoke.

I went quite often, when Derek was otherwise occupied,
and noted for him when the 'snoring' of the owlets began.
This was a hunger call, stimulating the adults to go hunting. It was a light, rhythmical sound which seemed to be
synchronised to the slow beating of my heart. When little
was happening, I had to fight hard to stay awake!

I shall never forget the first appearance of the cock bird,
which stood on a ledge like an apparition in white, staring
at the forest with eyes like black grapes set in a heart-
shaped facial disc, above the hooked beak that marked out
the bird as a predator. I watched the cock return across a
glade with shallow wingbeats, clutching a vole in its talons.
The calling of the young increased in volume and pitch.
One glorious night, young owls on their first flight alighted
on the roof of the hide. I looked up to see their claws—just a
few inches above my head!

Chapter 13

The High Roads

In the Dales, it is easy for a motorist to go mountaineering. I developed a love-hate relationship with Greenhow Hill, where the road from Grassington to Pateley Bridge crests at 1,323 feet. Love came first, in the form of a delightful character called Tommy Marshall, who took services in our Chapel and actually made us laugh. He spoke even more informally in the schoolroom on the following evening. The large building had filled with people anxious to listen to this evangelical preacher—this spiritual powerhouse in the guise of a dalesman 'off t'tops' who physically was 'nobbut t'size o' three pennorth o' copper'.

The posters announcing his visit mentioned 'Tommy Marshall of Greenhow Hill'. At one time I thought the placename was a synonym for heaven, especially as Tommy was fond of reminding us of its elevation. He told of the appointment of a young parson as vicar of Greenhow and the comment of one of his parishioners: 'Well! It's as near heaven as you'll ever get.'

I detested Greenhow when there were climatic excesses —a high wind, flurries of snow or, worse still, drifts of snow, and rain that, once begun, never seemed to know when to stop. I was returning late one night after giving a lecture on the Dales at Grantley Hall residential school near Ripon. Two-thirds of the way up the Banks, the car had an electrical failure. I walked to the nearest farm that sported a light. The door was opened by a farmer who had just had a bath, donned freshly-laundered pyjamas, supped a cup of coffee before a crackling fire and intended to go to bed. He did just that—as I struggled back to the car in a strong wind, muttering hard words about Greenhow.

Another day, when I was in better spirits, I took the road from Pateley Bridge to Greenhow and then found myself going from spring back to winter in a few minutes. Down in the town, a blackbird was carolling; up on Greenhow I heard the whistle of the golden plover, calling on bare ground between the cores of ancient snowdrifts. One of Kipling's 'soldiers three', stationed in an arid area of India, remembered Greenhow for its 'tewits'. I recall the lych-gate of Greenhow's burial ground. Carved on the gate are some familiar words: 'I will lift up mine eyes to the hills.' Here, you tend to look down on them!

Mist and drizzle may be experienced on Greenhow when the housewives of Pateley are hanging out washing, and yet when an autumn mist clogs Nidderdale the sun may be shining from a powder-blue sky on the folk who live on the Hill. Harald Bruff, who wrote about the doings of Greenhow folk, frequently referred to the wind, noting that it 'blows fresh and is laden with the fragrance of ling bloom, bent grass and wet moss, the true moor mixture.'

The name of the local inn, the Miner's Arms, hints at the main reason why this straddling village should have developed in the wilderness. This was part of a highly-mineralised tongue of land, from which over the centuries kings' ransoms in lead were lifted. At Greenhow, the houses are like stones on a necklace, with the main road as the thread. The settlement took shape in the seventeenth century, when miners who had trudged up the Banks from Nidderdale each working day were permitted to erect cottages on moorland 'intakes'. Some miners continued to walk, preferring a more sheltered setting for their homes.

A Victorian miner remembered by Fred Longhorn arrived on the Hill at 5-30 a.m. and rested for half-an-hour before joining the shift that began at 6 a.m. Fred's father, Oade Will, who died in 1933, used to take a horse and cart from Greenhow to Skipton to collect coal. He would set off from home at 5 a.m. and (fearing robbers), he usually slipped his money into his clogs.

Greenhow is a ghostly spot. George Gill, who at the time I joined *The Dalesman* was the proprietor of Stump Cross Caverns, which were 'open to view', told me of a night of full moon when some campers on Greenhow heard the sound of clogs on the nearby road at about midnight. Yet there was nobody to be seen. In 1939, when George was living in Duck Street at Greenhow, he heard the sound of clogs outside the house and noticed that the moon was at full. The clogs sounded on the gravel of the road, then on the cobblestones by its side, and finally on the gritstone slab at the door. Neither George nor his wife could see anyone.

At the time of the Luddite troubles in Lancashire, soldiers were force-marched from their base in Yorkshire to help quell the disturbances. A group of men trudged up the Greenhow road on such a hot day that one of their number, John Kay, had sunstroke. His friends bathed his head, but he died. He was buried by the road, and local people reared a stone at his head and feet to mark the spot. They also left a musket beside the body.

In subsequent years, Greenhowers had the habit, when passing the two upright stones, of 'danking' their clogs to make the metal ring, at the same time calling out, 'Gie us a knock, John Kay.' Fred Longthorn and others dug down and found the skeleton, together with some brass buttons. They sent a thigh bone to the doctor at Pateley Bridge for study, and he deduced that John Kay was an especially tall man. The grave was refilled with earth.

There was still an air of mystery about the spot. A group of Greenhow residents were returning home at 1 a.m., when strange sounds were reported by the womenfolk, who had walked ahead. The sounds came from the grave of John Kay. The men investigated. Fortunately it was a night of clear moonlight. They found a tramp had lain down to sleep, his head resting on the hummock of the grave. He was snoring!

Years ago, I asked a Wharfedale man about Park Rash, a

formidable brow on the connecting road between Wharfedale and Coverdale. 'Nay,' he said, 'there isn't much I can tell thee about it; it's nobbut a big hill.' I sensed there was much of interest. Hunter's Stone, a substantial pillar, was used as a guide post in monastic times. Much older is a ditch, Ta Dyke, believed to have been a defensive position in Brigantean times.

'Park' is a reference to an area set aside for red deer. In 1409, the Earl of Westmorland was granted a warren park, plus a lodge. 'Rash' means a steep hill. The road, which was given a hard surface as recently as 1953, is like a crinkled grey ribbon on the landscape. On the map is Diamond Hill. C. J. Cutcliffe Hyne, the novelist, who lived at Kettlewell, panned for gold in some of these streams and found it, but in minuscule quantities that hardly repaid him for his effort. Lead was mined in these grey limestone hills.

Local men have told me of early motor traffic—of the Whit Monday endurance race between London and Newcastle, which was routed over Park Rash. Kit Wiseman and another man stationed themselves near the steepest section, with two horses and chains, and prepared to tow out any luckless competitors. When motor cycles were tested here in the 1920s, many of the machines came to a shuddering halt on loose stones. An exception was that ridden by Alec Jackson, of Keighley, who usually stood on the saddle of his motor cycle as he began his rapid climb. 'Folk used to fair gape at him.' Viewed from the Kettlewell side, the line of the ancient route looks like a symbol for lightning, tacked to the fellside. Harry Plews, of West Park Farm, told me of some of the drivers of large loads who, taking a wrong turn in Wensleydale, found themselves negotiating a road more suited to the Andes. The Plews family were startled to see an articulated vehicle of 32 tons going down empty. A 'West Yorkshire' bus that had been conveying cavers to the area was reversed into one of their fields while turning. In 1970, a diesel road roller ran away backwards and demolished a wall.

Incidents during the winter of 1978–79 have passed into

local folklore. Park Rash was blocked for about three months, and snow accumulated to the height of the telephone wires. The youth hostel warden at Kettlewell, having—of all things—a handbook on how to construct igloos, decided to do just that. He built an igloo on Park Rash, using blocks of snow cut from the drifts. The work was carried out on a day of clear blue skies but in such low temperature that the snow seemed almost as substantial as brick.

At West Park Farm, in that white winter, the road was blocked on Christmas Eve; it became reasonably clear for a week in March and was finally opened up on April 3. Four days later, the Plews family received a first load of hay from Coverdale.

The Buttertubs Pass, between Wensleydale and Swaledale, is not the most exacting moorland crossing in the Dales but it is the one that most visitors remember best. The road has an appeal of alpine character, a high summit and a most curious name. At the Buttertubs, a traveller climbs for over 900 feet from Hawes and makes a steep descent of nearly 800 feet to the valley of the Swale. I once crossed in the grandfather of all thunderstorms—and felt extremely vulnerable as lightning flashed from clouds as blue-black as Stephen's ink. On hot, clear days, the eyes range over ridge upon ridge in this lean landscape, to where a Sphinx-like Ingleborough demands to be admired. The local fells, Great Shunner and Lovely Seat, have soft-vowelled names; they belie the harsh situation.

I once mentioned Buttertubs to Kit Calvert, of Hawes, and saw his weather-seamed face light up with pleasure. He was remembering a wagonette crossing on Muker Show Day, 75 years before. The outfit belonged to Elijah Allen, who hired it out to all-comers. When the upward gradients were encountered, the passengers had to get out and walk. Kit, a lay preacher, took services at Keld chapel during one inclement wartime winter. On foggy nights, he motored over Buttertubs slowly, with the driver's window down and his head protruding from the car. Wartime lighting meant that the headlamp beam was weak. Kit was listening, as he drove, for the sound of wheels against pebbles, which meant he had driven off the road, which in places is no more than a ledge cut from the fellside.

A broadcaster stood with a farmer beside the Buttertubs Pass and looked around him. He saw the ranges of fells, like great waves in a petrified sea. 'What is the name for this wonderful tract of countryside?' he asked the farmer, who replied, simply and with flattened vowels, 'Buttertubs.' The visitor had expected a very grand name.

The Buttertubs, shafts in limestone, lie within a few yards of the road. Years ago, a warden of the National Park parked his car and was eating his mid-day snack when he heard a rumbling sound. A piece of land collapsed, revealing yet another 'buttertub', which he duly reported to the council in Hawes, who put a rope around it until some more permanent barrier could be arranged. A hoary tale concerns the visitors who asked a farmer the depth of one of the shafts, only to be told, 'That's bottomless.' The farmer pointed to another shaft and said, 'Yan's deeper still!'

Yet another story insists that the name Buttertubs comes from a custom of using the cool shafts as a store for butter in hot weather, which is an unlikely tale. Perhaps the explanation is prosaic—that the shafts look like the containers used for supplying butter in bulk to the grocer. The average depth is 58 feet. The man who ran sheep in this area when I first knew it kept a rope handy for the times when sheep slid into the buttertubs and must be rescued.

I know worse stretches of road in the Dales than the Buttertubs Pass. A local example is the approach to Tan Hill from Keld—a road that crosses the bridge below Wainwath Falls, swings this way and that as it negotiates a steep bank and eventually adopts a kindly gradient beyond West Stonesdale. Buttertubs, however, has a special appeal in its name. There is a curiosity value in the down-to-earth if unromantic title of 'Buttertubs'.

Chapter 14

Magic Lanterns

Bob Swallow, who has an aptitude for audio-visual presentations, sent out invitations to the 'world première' of a tribute to the Settle-Carlisle railway, in pictures, words and music. The only old-fashioned aspect of that evening, for which he booked the village institute, was the food, none of which had been bought in a supermarket. As a long-time enthusiast for the famous line by which the old Midland company claimed a direct share of the lucrative Scottish traffic, I had seen many a slide show about it.

The extravaganza produced by a Preston man, must have taken him to the limits of concentration, for he used a battery of projectors, several screens standing side by side, a tape-recording of words and music, an overworked wife and, doubtless, a bottle of nerve tonic. I could not really concentrate on the subject for looking at the producer as, working from a script, he kept the intricate show in progress.

The technical wizardry called audio-visual, which means that once set in motion the production is untouched by hand, reminds me of my own experiences of picture shows in the Dales. My earliest memory is of attending a weekly meeting at the Salvation Army Citadel in Skipton. Scores of children were entertained by what was then called a 'magic lantern'. We were suitably impressed, though the slides were of goody-goody types to whom we could not really relate. Why did we go? Every child received a bag of sweets at the end of the performance. One of my first jobs at the *Craven Herald* was to attend the weekly slide show of the

Craven Naturalists and Scientific Association in an impressively decadent lecture theatre at the Science and Art School. Sufferers from vertigo were led blindfolded to the lower rows of seats. The lofty room had lots of shadowy corners, draped with cobwebs, which gave the place a sense of mystery. (All was to be lost when it was gutted and the space incorporated in characterless modern rooms illuminated by the cold glare of strip lighting.)

I recall the wartime austerity, the dimmed streetlights, the dingy furnishings within the Victorian building and, when my eyes had grown accustomed to the gloom of the Lecture Theatre, the sprinkling of members of the Association. Some of the men looked as though they had been taken down from shelves and dusted. Almost without exception, they were small in stature, wearing dark suits, with starched shirts, ties and tie-pins. The women were, by and large, unconcerned about their appearance, having short hair, tweedy clothes and sensible, sometimes men's-type, shoes on their feet. It was a splendid fellowship of naturalists, many of whom were experts in their chosen fields, from birds to butterflies and from mammals to mosses.

In that pre-television, monochromatic age, the meetings of the Craven Naturalists brought some glamour into our lives. We saw 'lantern lectures' of distant places; we were introduced to the wonders of nature and our own glorious Dales countryside. Nature was the concern of Mr Grist, of Leeds University, who before speaking about Bird Migration announced to a large crowd, and a most embarrassed reporter, 'If a representative of *The Times*—or, er, *The Craven Herald & Pioneer*—is present, he may be interested to know that I will have some notes available after the lecture.' It seems that Mr Grist had so often been misquoted by junior reporters that he prepared a resumé of his lecture. It ensured accuracy—and more newspaper space was devoted to it.

Frederic Riley, the Settle naturalist and antiquary, offered us pictures of our own Craven district. I recall in particular his 'Ribble from its Source to the Sea'. The 'lantern' was an imposing object, with brass attachments. Originally it had been illuminated by 'lime light', operated by first taking the upright mantle from the nearest gas point and connecting its flame to a stream of oxygen from a rope-covered cylinder on the floor. You could actually smell the lantern. Sometimes it glowed red hot and on one occasion—so Mr Riley told me—a projector of this type had to be carried out on a shovel. When adapted for electricity, it ran so hot you might have boiled a kettle on it!

I recognised in Frederic Riley—this lean, grey-haired man of the hills—an authority on Dales life. He showed us slides of places that were no more than 40 miles away but then seemed unbelievably distant. He had actually climbed some of the hills. And because he hand-tinted his pictures, there was colour, albeit garish. One lecture included an impression of the fiery light of a setting sun on the Stone Men (cairns) at the summit of Gragareth. Someone, emotionally overcame by the colourful effect, showed appreciation of this particular slide by clapping: the applause was taken up and lasted for at least a minute.

Frederic Riley's good friend, Eddie Horner, often projected the slides. I had some long chats with Eddie during my early days with *The Dalesman* and heard entertaining stories of his family association with photography—an association that began in 1858, when his uncle, Michael Horner, set up a shop in the Market Place after going to Manchester to learn the trade. Those were the days when a photographer needed a handcart if he visited the rural areas: the camera was a bulky item. There was no shutter, a cap being removed from the lens for the given exposure. The 'wet plate' process was used. A plate was exposed while wet and had to be developed (in a special lightproof tent, on a tripod) before it could dry out. The chemical process was somewhat harmful to the operator but gave a lasting negative.

We published some of the Horner pictures in the magazine. The choice was considerable. Ladies wore crinolines, men had sternly-cut suits with drainpipe trousers and little boys had petticoats, for they were not 'breeched' until the age of three or four. The girls who appeared in the Victorian family groups had the most wonderful embroidered frocks with frills, their legs being encased in black stockings. Daylight was the only form of illumination in the studio and an exposure of eight or ten seconds was common. The subject must remain perfectly still and a metal fork, shaped like a letter U, was used as a head rest for long exposures. Frederic Riley told me that he 'wore' such a fork when he was photographed as a lad wearing a sailor suit. The ends of the fork showed on either side of his head but were painted out on the plate!

Richard Kearton and his brother Cherry, natives of Thwaite in Swaledale, were pioneer wildlife photographers and early popularisers of natural history. On the death of Frank Lowe, the Bolton naturalist, in 1985, I inherited the letters of encouragement and advice about 'lantern lecturing' that Frank had received from Richard Kearton in the period 1924 to 1927, the last letter being penned a few months before Kearton died. He was an outstanding exponent of the art of lecturing with pictures in public.

In February, 1924, Richard acknowledged Frank's letter inquiring about the cost of a slide show.

> For an ordinary slide lecture I will charge you £8.8.0 if I happen to be in your neighbourhood doing other work and if I have to come specially £9.9.0. Please keep these quotations to yourself as far as possible as my usual fee in the North is £10.10.0. It will perhaps be better to confine the lecture to members of your different photography clubs so as to keep down expenses. If you rope in 400 people there ought to be no fear of making a loss.

Was Richard himself becoming rich through his efforts? He wrote to Frank Lowe in May, 1924, 'Opinions about your humble servant are divided. One half the people conclude I'm mad and the other half that I'm making a fortune out of my job. Neither correct, although both expressed with much confidence.'

Letters reveal his flair for novelty. Richard's wife coloured some of his slides; he himself could not relate how the effects were achieved, 'and doubt if she could herself without writing a Volume about it. She used to be an artist & I suppose the fact has something to do with the effects she produces.' Kearton was wholeheartedly a slide lecturer. He wrote in February, 1925, 'Slow motion pictures may be quite good for a scientific demonstration but I do not think much of them for a popular audience and feel very glad I never spent £400 on a Camera to take them. My wife dislikes the things intensely. Moving pictures of any sort have had their day . . .' It is tempting to quote extensively from the letters, but I will restrict myself to a single sentence from one written in August, 1925, in which Richard noted, 'Don't lecture for nothing. It is as bad to pauperise the mind as the body.'

At *The Dalesman* we initiated a series of free lectures about Yorkshire: it was part of our plan to make the magazine better known. Mercifully, with only two of us concerned, it was not necessary to have a committee meeting or to re-state policy. Harry Scott, leaning back in his chair at coffee time, reached for his pipe, recharged it with his favourite Tom Long tobacco and said we might spend more time at the Women's Institutes. He reckoned that as women actually paid the newspaper and magazine bill every week, they were the people to contact. The lectures would be free, but travelling expenses might be charged if distances were great. At that time neither of us had a car: we relied on the taxi service run by an ever-cheerful Tommy Hargreaves of Newby.

I soon discovered that 'we' meant 'I'. Harry Scott had given lots of lectures in the past but was increasingly spending more time by the fire, with pipe and book. He did enjoy impromptu slide shows at his home, with a few invited friends, some nattering before and after the show and a snack supper to follow. It was all very cosy on winter evenings. Less cosy was the business of setting out with a heavy wooden box containing heavy glass-mounted slides of Yorkshire, of spending an hour or two on buses and having the trauma of setting up equipment in rooms with 'frost pictures' on the windows.

This happened in the Aire Valley. I left it to local people to provide the 'magic lantern', but on this occasion it had not been done. An old man believed there was 'one o' them picture things' in a lumber room. He was right. The dust of ages rose from the 'Glory Hole' (the traditional repository for junk, originally Chapel junk, being the space beneath the pulpit). The lantern was brought forth, dusted down and a socket found under a loose floorboard. We plugged in. I left it to one of the others to do this work when the old man said the ''lectrics want seeing to.' A light came on, followed by a murky image from the slide—the sort of image over which Baird rejoiced when first he demonstrated his ability to transmit television pictures. The old man sniffed and pronounced that the trouble was 'condensation'. I am not sure just when we actually recognised detail on a picture—perhaps it was a third of the way through—but by the end of the show we were grateful for the warmth generated by that rusty 'magic lantern'.

A Methodist minister caused problems when I acquired an old lantern of my own and took it to Hetton chapel. The place was packed. All was set up. The minister, noticing someone at the other end of the room, smiled broadly, extended his right hand in anticipation of a hand-clasp and advanced, oblivious of the electric cable that stretched across the floor. I recall looking at the lantern, of seeing the cable tighten as the minister tripped over it. The back of the lantern shot up and the bulb on its carriage shot out like a greyhound from a trap, and bounced several times before coming to rest. We had to use an ordinary bulb—and, like St Paul, saw through a glass darkly.

At Skipton a bulb exploded, and while the large congregation sang hymns I went on an expedition, looking for a replacement. Half an hour later I returned in triumph. The singing had continued, but now the members of the congregation, their voiceboxes raw, were croaking like frogs.

Another time, I occupied a famous old lecture theatre at the Science and Art School in Skipton. I handed over my slides to the Naturalists' projectionist, Alfred Hyde, little realising the power of the bulb in the large 'lantern'. Most of the slides were of the old-fashioned kind, being virtually unaffected by heat, but colour film was now becoming plentiful and I had mounted several transparencies, including a study of the Red Roofs of Whitby. As I spoke about Whitby, I noticed the Red Roofs bubbling in the heat.

I travelled to Yorkshire societies at Edinburgh and Aberystwyth. The Scottish gathering was connected with the University, the Welsh in a University town which on that occasion ran high with nationalist zeal. The relatively few Yorkshire folk gathered in a quiet room and sang 'Ilkla' Moor' with gusto, though with little hope of drowning out Welsh strains.

Harry Scott had agreed to go to Edinburgh, but the fireside exerted too great a pull when, in that 1963 winter, the Dales were blotted out with snow and, rumour had it, both the Settle-Carlisle line and the Waverley route, from Carlisle to Edinburgh, were virtually blocked. Would I take his appointment? With Settle station closed, I drove my battered Ford to Hellifield and entrained for the Lancaster-Carlisle. The view from the windows was whiteness, relieved only by the occasional black form of a tree and some disconsolate rooks. For most of this day and the next, the railway sleepers were snow-covered. The only green fields I saw lay near the Solway. The direct route to Edinburgh was, indeed, blocked, and as we moved on to Glasgow, the sides of cuttings were filling in with drifts that arched over to run frozen fingers along the sides of the carriages.

I changed trains at Glasgow and arrived in Edinburgh chilled and dispirited, with a dress suit belonging to Harry Scott which looked reasonable after I had borrowed half a dozen safety pins in lieu of needle and thread. Next morning, the only rail link between Scotland and England was that on the East Coast. I changed at York and again at Leeds. The rhythmic drumming of wheels against track seemed to have been with me for half my life when I eventually disembarked at Hellifield after a huge circular journey.

Next morning, Harry Scott came into the office in his carpet slippers, held his hands over the stove, rubbed them together, beamed and asked, 'Good journey to Edinburgh?' I was about to tell him when the telephone rang . . .

The lectures we gave about the Dales were never solemn. Harry Scott based his on six lines which he had pencilled on a card many years before, each line representing the characteristic of a Dalesman—realism, taciturnity, honesty, generosity, thrift and love for the native heath. Taciturnity was summed up as 'the ability to say nowt for a long time'. Like the jokes used by the comedians who went on the rounds of the music halls, the stories told by Harry lasted for many years. I inherited them and told them with equal success until, in recent times, the appreciation of old Dales tales changed, in all but the most rural of places. Speed and slickness became desirable aspects of humour.

The Dalesman became a part of 'jam and Jerusalem', as someone summed up the Women's Institute movement. Harry Scott told with merriment how he was introduced by someone deputising for the president: 'She is on holiday . . . how we all wish we were with her.' With this, the speaker stood up! He was amused during the often boring business meeting that preceded a talk to hear the minutes of the previous meeting being read out, including: 'It was decided to get some more copies of "Jerusalem" as it was considered that the words we had were dirty.'

Before attending one meeting, I called in to see a farmer friend, who asked, 'Nah then, where's ta going?' Said I, 'To talk to the ladies of the Women's Institute.' He said, 'There are no ladies in the Women's Institute.' I waited for him to continue, as I knew he would. 'No ladies—just girls, young girls and old girls!' That evening I did not have to think hard about how to introduce the talk.

There were the grand occasions, too, though when I first went to give a talk at Saltaire to help raise money for old folks' charities, I took along with me our modest projector and a yard or two of flex. The meeting was to be held in the Town Hall, which I reached at the time it was being invaded by hundreds of people. Having parked my car a third of a mile away, I walked to Sir Titus Salt's imposing hall, passing between carvings of stone lions which, according to local tradition, were originally intended for the Nelson monument in Trafalgar Square. I stood in the foyer of the hall, surrounding by chattering people. Eventually I asked one of them about the attraction. Was it all-in wrestling? Or mass bingo? 'There's a chap coming to talk to us about t'Dales,' was the reply, and I felt the blood drain from my head.

It was a great 'do', with about 600 people in attendance. At the front, I was provided with all sorts of electrical gadgets: I had never seen my slides projected on a larger scale. Somehow, I managed to keep talking. The *Dalesman* jokes must have got through, because I was asked to go back another year.

Setting up for a slide show was often the most entertaining part of the evening. None was stranger than in the spring of 1976, when an epidemic of Settle-Carlislitis spread through the Dales. Those who were infected became delirious: they had glazed eyes, fevered brows and a proneness to rant. This complaint afflicted thousands of people, all of them railway enthusiasts. For in May, 1976, was celebrated the centenary of the opening to passenger traffic of the famous Settle-Carlisle railway.

I was asked to give a slide show on the railway, and I suggested it might take place, with permission, in the waiting room of Settle station. On the previous evening, I took my equipment along to test it out—and discovered what I should have known: that the station was not electrified. An electrician loaned me a considerable length of flex, which I extended from the waiting room, along the guttering of the main buildings, across to the former Stationmaster's house and into the kitchen, where a suitable socket was found. It was a winter event, and I had misused prayer by asking for dull weather. In the event, the Almighty provided clear skies, but the operatic society loaned me lengths of curtaining. After the lecture, four of us chatted about the possibility of observing the centenary. The station had been electrified before our ambitious project was developed.

* * *

I reckon that over the years I have given almost 2,000 slide shows. My diary fills with appointments, sometimes three a week. Dalesfolk are cunning in the way they ask for help, first mentioning some person or subject of mutual interest and then working their way deviously to the main topic—a free talk.

Occasionally, I do not jot down enough information in my diary. One entry—'Settle-Carlisle'. Temperance Hall, 7.30—troubled me for a week or two, for I could not recall whether it was a request for a lecture, or whether someone had told me of one I might consider attending. And where was the Temperance Hall? When the day came, I was no wiser. At 7.30, or thereabouts, I decided to have a bath. The hot water seemed to boil when my wife took a telephone call from 'somebody who says you should be giving a lecture at the Temperance Hall'.

For some reason, I had associated the venue with Keighley. As I made my dripping way to the telephone, I tried to assess how long I would take to reach the town. Then a bright Dales voice announced that this Temperance Hall was at Keasden—only six miles away! How could I have forgotten one of my favourite venues, a converted barn, at the edge of the moor; a building full of character, where years ago the electricity supply was brought by cable run out from the hall to a socket in the garage of the nearest farm, and where the patrons sat on forms. I suggested they might serve the supper first and I would be with them in half an hour. At the start of my lecture, I apologised to them, and also to my left foot, which I had been about to wash when the telephone call was received!

Chapter 15

Forest of Bowland

To the west of Clapham lay Burnmoor—a heathery ridge, wind-smoothed and almost treeless. On March days, the gamekeepers would fire selected areas of the moor to burn off the rank growth and encourage new shoots, food for grouse and sheep. Seeing the blue smoke rising as I went about my business in the village, I thought of it as something akin to incense, burnt to appease a god of nature.

The map proclaimed 'Forest of Bowland'. Was the land beyond the heather ridge some sort of annexe to Sherwood Forest? The local council seemed to have lent support to this notion through a headpiece on the signposts—a white circular plate featuring the outline of a chubby little bowman in the act of drawing his bow.

I looked for thatched wooden houses and saw instead some handsome stone-and-slate structures—minor halls and seventeenth-century farmsteads, with mullioned windows and porches decorated with the initials of the proud folk who had built them. I sniffed the air, expecting it to be flavoured by venison being cooked, but the moorland breeze carried only the tang of peat. The first Bowland Forester I met was a typical farmer of the period, complete with cap and clogs. I asked him about Bowland. He snapped, 'It's Bolland, lad!' It was said to mean 'land of cattle', a reference to the medieval vaccaries or cattle ranches, established in cleared areas of the old forest.

I crossed the ridge by Bowland Knotts. The road makes a bold, frontal attack on the moor, ignoring the whims of local topography, passing through the realms of tewit and curlew to those of red grouse and golden plover. An old man had recalled when the highway was little more than a rough track, with grass growing up the centre. He also told me that the wooden shooting box, the meeting place of sportsmen in August, had a division so that the social classes did not mix. He was distinctly working-class, hired for the day as a beater. Food was sent up from a hotel at Austwick. One year, beef but no bread was delivered by horse and trap. 'We had sandwiches, though. We put a bit o' fat in between two pieces of lean beef!'

When I first went Bowland way, and began the long descent into the upper valley of the Hodder, most of the landscape was open, though all but a few farms were desolate, forming part of the catchment area for Stocks Reservoir. The Forestry Commission had permission to plant conifers, but these and other modern forests were little more than a stubble on Bowland's chin.

There was still scope for the short-eared owls that came in each February to entertain us with their nuptial display of wing-clapping; they also tested our wits if we decided to look for a nest. A friend who recorded the sounds of wildlife was delighted one April dawn to swing his parabolic reflector over an arc and pick up black grouse hissing and cooing in no less than five places.

Sparrow hawks nesting in the larch plantations spread a reign of terror over a wide area and collected whinchats from the moor's edge, as I discovered when I found a plucking stone beside a forest road. The male had rough-dressed the prey before calling down the female. Hearing the coarse shouting of a carrion crow, I looked up to find it harrying a gentle buzzard. After dark, I would occasionally hear the scream of a barn owl, the hooting of the male brown owl and the rousing 'kewick' of its mate, a sound often heard when the young of the year were being persuaded to leave the parental territory and find niches of their own.

I went to the new Gisburn Forest looking for birds. There were 'vole years', when the coarse herbage of the rides and glades held innumerable runs of short-tailed field voles, a basic food for owls and kestrels; the birds swallowed them whole and then littered their nesting areas with pellets composed of hair and bones, indigestible portions of the prey. At times I heard the squeaking of voles at almost every footfall. A kestrel nest above the door of a derelict barn was lagged with such material.

I became friendly with a forester, Percy Tilbury, his wife and family. I tended to think of the children living at this old farmstead, in the middle of a thickly afforestated area, as Children of the New Forest. Percy, who also rented and farmed a few fields, proved to be an excellent naturalist, with a regard for the welfare of the local fauna. It was Percy who invited me to listen to the 'whistling deer'.

I came across my first deer 'slots' with something of the excitement of Robinson Crusoe discovering the footprint of Man Friday. I had been out in the forest for hours, watching birds. In a moist area were the fresh prints of mammalian feet. Had they been made by sheep? I knew that in some of the big northern spruce forests lived sheep that managed to avoid being included in the periodical 'gatherings' by the farmers and were semi-wild. I was also aware that Bowland sheep, being mainly 'half-bred 'uns', were huge compared with the little horned sheep of the high fells.

I explored further. A sharp, clear whistle broke the silence. It came from a creature that stood perhaps 15 yards ahead. I 'froze' and listened to a sequence of whistles of a type I had never heard before. They were not uniform in pitch or duration, some being little more than birdy chirps. Whatever had produced the strange sounds moved off noisily through the dense growth.

I had actually heard the alarm calls of a sika deer. The sharp squeal, nasal in character, was like a whistle when heard distantly. The deer in that Bowland forest were descendants of beasts that had evolved in the forests of Asia, being brought to Britain to adorn a gentleman's estate, and to Bowland to provide sport for staghounds.

That autumn, I stood in Percy Tilbury's farmyard at what

the Pennine folk picturesquely call 'the edge o' dark', and waited (in vain) for more whistling—this time from a territorial stag. The Bowland sika originated from a small number emparked near Gisburn. These were carted to the hunting ground, to be recaptured and returned to the park at the end of the day. Naturally, some deer objected to such treatment and made good their escape. When I first began studying the deer, the numbers were beginning to build up and stags were discovering the fellside forests where there was sanctuary and, for the moment, a considerable area of good grazing.

Sika are medium-sized deer. The male (stag) looks as though it has been assembled from bits and pieces of other deer, having the clean, branched antlers of the red deer, the dimensions of the fallow and the prominent type of caudal disc of the roe (though whereas the sika's white rump patch is heart-shaped, the roe's has the shape of a kidney). The winter coat is dark, the summer coat a gleaming chestnut, well dappled. Stags cast their antlers in spring, grow replacements with great rapidity, move back into the company of the hinds, or females, as summer wanes and, in September, go through the ritual of the rut, as the mating season is known.

I heard the territorial whistles of a stag from near Percy's home when I revisited the area a few days later. The crowing of the cock pheasants died away as the birds went to roost. Parent tawny owls conversed with each other about the future of their offspring. Suddenly, the air shivered with the sikine whistling. Three loud, clear whistles followed in orderly sequence—each starting off low, rising in pitch and tailing off smoothly, in a lovely crescent of sound. I might have been listening to the piping of a northern Pan.

Another evening, standing among the trees, with the wind fanning my face—not the back of my neck, so that I did not offer my scent to the deer—the calling of a stag was so close the shock seemed to put ice particles in my bloodstream. I saw the beast moving by the faint light from the orange glare of street lights in a town a dozen miles away.

It was the start of 20 years of Bowland deer-watching. The Forest was so large and dense that a deer had only to take two paces to the right to lose itself in thick cover. Now and again I 'glassed' deer from a distance as they grazed in sunlit rides. I became an expert on crotties (deer droppings!), studying them when, in the rich grazing days of summer, they formed an amorphous mass, and in winter when they were dark and compacted. That particular study ended when a doctor friend pointed out that the calibre of a dropping was simply that of the small gut and that some of my Bowland half-bred sheep were capable of parting with crotties that were almost as large as those of a deer!

I met a host of characters living in the dale country of this western outlier of the Pennines, which I was soon to think of as 'welly-country', for the glaciers had generously smeared it with boulder clay up to an elevation of about 600 feet. Now and again I had my wellingtons plucked from my feet by the first grip of clay that recent rain had given the consistency of Yorkshire pudding mixture. The deer loved it. During the rut a stag would wallow in the wettest areas of the woods and clamber back to its feet as filthy as a Rugby forward, leaving a smooth, saucer-shaped hollow bearing the marks of its cleaves and antlers, for it had a compunction to leave its mark by pressing the hard antler against the rim.

By day, the deer lay up in old woodland adorning the sides of gills, the water-carved valleys that began modestly on the moors and increased in size as they reached lower ground, terminating where the becks that occupied them spilled their cold waters into the mighty Ribble, in the shadow of Pendle Hill. The indomitable farmers of this part of Bowland had learnt to cope with the problems of a predominantly wet climate. Wellies were obligatory. A farmer who injured his leg had it put in plaster at the hospital, where the doctor told him not to get it wet for umpteen days. So he adapted two of the modern farmer's best friends—a plastic fertiliser bag and some used binder twine—and swathed his leg in this waterproof material.

When antique dealers showed interest in brass bed-heads, these no longer appeared in the hedges. One man with several hedge gaps tackled, instead, the large tup that occupied the main field, fitting a hazel rod to its curved horns. The tup could no longer get through the gap—and its deportment while holding the rod steady was soon like that of a top model.

In what I came to think of as 'mid' Bowland—the intermediate land between the high moors and the sylvan valley of the Ribble—I wandered in a landscape decked with the remnants of the old Forest, with rowan and ash, hazel and holly. These survivors clung to the sides of the gills and were so common around the fields that, viewed from a distance, the area appeared to be lightly wooded.

A medieval flavour was imparted by names like Ox Pasture, which I entered to study the wallows of the sika stags in autumn. Presumably, centuries ago, the oxen used for ploughing were kept here, at the edge of the moor, where water seeped into the beck through indigenous woodland and the area was of little value. In Ox Pasture, trees grew where they would. Fallen timber remained on the ground until it rotted, and meanwhile it yielded big white grubs, food for the green woodpeckers. The maniacal laughter of the woodpeckers resounded in the wood each spring.

I parked my car in Forest Becks, chatted with the farmer at Fooden and, when glancing at the map, came across Fat Hill, Ouzel Hall, Cow House Hill and Windy Pike. The farmers were just beginning to abandon the old ways: they were mechanised, but 'nobbut just'. During a spell of haytime, when 'drinkings' were served, I pondered on the history of the field in which we sat eating scones and drinking hot, mid-brown tea.

'Wouldn't it be good to know about all the people who've made hay in this field?' I said, and let my mind drift down the centuries . . .

The farmer slaked his thirst and said, 'I can tell you

—ivvery one of 'em.' I had never thought of him as a historian. 'There's been me and me Dad.'

When 'Dad' took over the farm, the field that now yielded a good crop of hay had been simply pasture, with that coarse grass called 'bent' and so many rushes that Aunt Mary, while riding her pony, had lost her bonnet among the 'rush bobs' and never did find it! Already, there was ploughing and reseeding. The hares and the sika deer converged in the fields that greened up weeks ahead of those round about. I once counted 30 brown hares in one five-acre plot. Within a few years, the landscape had changed dramatically and become a hedge-to-hedge expanse of lush ryegrass. The old haytime gave way to silage-making.

It was Jimmy Dinsdale who provided me with an introduction to 'mid' Bowland. I met him one evening as he leaned on a gate, surveying his land. We yarned about the Dales—he was born in Upper Wharfedale—and Mrs Dinsdale provided a cup of tea. Jimmy kept me informed about the movement of the deer. Both he and they were surprisingly tolerant. Half a dozen fine stags were spending their daytimes lying in one of his best meadows.

I walked along the hedgeside, just inside an adjacent field. When I thought he must have been mistaken, for there were no deer in view, the stags rose in all the glory of their summer coats. So close had they been lying, they might have sprung out of the ground. I noticed the plummy hue of the 'velvet', the tough hairy skin that covers the partly-grown antlers.

My studies of sika deer advanced rapidly through the help of two fine naturalists—John Robinson and Keith Briggs. With John I wrote papers for *Deer*, the magazine of the British Deer Society. With Keith, I studied the vocabulary of sika, using parabolic reflector, microphone and tape recorder. He came to Bowland after recording the sounds made by adders, Britain's only poisonous species of snake, and with a tale of a friend who startled a gamekeeper.

Aircraft noises were the bane of a recordist's life, and so

this man was inclined to go out when few aircraft stirred. He had found from experience that early on Sunday morning was usually quiet. He ventured among the rhododendrons of a local estate. When he had secured some bird recordings, though full light had not yet come, the naturalist rejoined the path, holding the reflector up to his face and looking at the world through the small hole used for sighting. The gamekeeper appeared unexpectedly. A look of horror crossed his face and he fled, not having previously seen a big silver dish on legs.

I hasten to add that many gamekeepers were friendly and helped in our work. Now and again, we came across the testy variety, and one such man had a beat that took in some prime deer country. At the time of rut, when the air filled strange sikine noises, I met Keith and we ventured onto his land.

A harvest moon had a retinue of bright stars and the windless conditions were ideal for recording. We looked down on the favourite grazing area of the sika deer—and saw only mist, white and dense, like cotton wool. Keith assembled his recording equipment and handed me a spare set of headphones. He slowly moved the reflector, then held it firm as it picked up the sounds made by a sexually-excited stag. Previously, we had heard only the most obvious outbursts, but this stag was rarely quiet, and the range of sound was impressive, including peevish wailing, grunts, clicks and in due course the startling squeals that from a distance sounded like whistles.

For half an hour, with subtle movements of the reflector, we followed the stag about, recording other stags and sensing the fervour of the rut though we could see nothing for the mist. The session ended not because the deer went quiet, but on the appearance nearby of half a dozen hinds. We had not seen them approach. They were unsure what to make of us but were suspicious. The old hind gave an alarm squeal. With the gamekeeper's house a quarter of a mile away, we retreated. Later, in a lay-by, we played over part of the recording, hoping it would stimulate other stags into lusty calling. It did no such thing—but the tawny owls seemed more excited than usual.

It was while helping Jack Shuttleworth in the hayfield that I heard of a pet calf at the next farm, New Ing. My inclination was immediately to throw down my rake and leap over the fence separating us from New Ing, but having had 'drinkings', complete with strawberries and cream and the odd can of shandy, I continued with haytiming until the shades had lengthened, hedgehogs were lumbering across the newly-shorn meadows and the tawny owls were active. Sometime during the night, a curtain of cloud was drawn across the district. I could visit New Ing knowing there would be no haytime to interrupt.

The sika calf had been named Bambi, and Bambi was growing up as one of the Hodgson family, which consisted of Arthur, his wife Doreen, their daughter Adele and Doreen's mother, Nan. They hailed from the northern dales—from Teesdale and the upper Eden Valley—and it was a delight to chat with them about Dales life. Arthur's passion for wildlife, his routine as a farmer, and his many and varied hobbies, such as stick-carving, ensured that the New Ing routine was rarely dull.

Bambi had been born early in July, when Arthur went to mow a meadow. Grass began to tumble in neat swathes as the cutter-bar attached to the tractor chattered away. The denizens of the meadow—hares, rabbits, pheasants and curlews—scuttered for safety. Arthur left his machine to attend to a delinquent part. As he glanced ahead, he noticed the head of a deer calf showing above the as yet unmown grass. Arthur moved the wee creature to one side and resumed his mowing. On the following day, the calf was found again. It was chilled and thin. The Hodgsons promptly adopted it.

Bambi was to transform our lives. She would enter the farmhouse and eat such undeerlike food as sweets and orange peel, and she was to give us an insight into the more tender aspects of sikine life, for she presided over a growing family. Arthur had the unorthodox idea of taking her into the countryside to meet a stag. Some people scoffed at the notion—but it worked. When Bambi was in season and giving a kittenish mewing, she was placed in the back of the Land-Rover and taken to a tract of woodland with a resident stag. She was then released.

Would she be served? In the presence of the stag, Bambi became so excited that the hair of her coat and the long hairs of the caudal disc stood out. She moved towards the stag with the high-stepping gait of a hackney. The stag at first recoiled, possibly because of the cloying human scent, but then Bambi was served. When Arthur called, she returned to him. In due course, a calf was born.

Her first calf was Kiki, the second Heidi, the third Kochi. Kiki was born in a dry shed, part of a group of outbuildings lying some 100 yards from the farmhouse. A weak light was left burning, and when the birth-time was near, Arthur kept his eye on progress by looking through a small hole in the door. Bambi parted with her calf and the Hodgson family, roused from their beds, walked through the summer night to witness the calf get to its feet and suckle milk—a process which Arthur called 'tittying'.

I, too, became familiar with the sight of new-born calves, which at first were to be seen in sheds and were then delivered by Bambi in secluded parts of the little deer park. Sika was autumn's youngster, born on the last day of September. By great good fortune I visited the farm within half an hour of her birth and I sat in the croft, watching her being cleaned up by Bambi, who then suckled her offspring. Rays of strong sunlight slanted from a sky which, by its colours and interesting cloud patterns, would have delighted Walt Disney.

The growing herd had its normal grazing supplemented by acorns and other countryside fruits; we were able to watch the casting of the winter coat and the assumption of the summer pelage of dappled chestnut. Then it was the time of the rut again, and the strange whistles of amorous sika stags could be heard.

And so it went on, till Bambi was a plump matron,

presiding over a large family. At the time of the rut, a wild stag would oblige by leaping into the deer enclosure at the farm. Eventually Bambi died, but her genetic stock persists in Bowland.

Chapter 16

Beyond Hell Gill

I came to think of the area beyond Hell Gill as 'The Big Country'. My favourite time for a visit was when daffodils were flowering at the roadside—and when patches of snow lingered in the ancient joints of the fells. At Hell Gill, I continued to think of the area as it was before the boundary changes of 1974, for this limestone ravine, the cradle of the river Eden, marked the demarcation between the North Riding of Yorkshire and Westmorland. In the good old days, I would cross the lean lands between Brough and Middleton, rejoicing that Yorkshire claimed one bank of the upper Tees.

My justification for including the area in *The Dalesman* was that here was prime dales country, beyond the range of commuters and not yet popular with weekend cottagers. A stranger, hearing of a place called Hell Gill, would doubtless think of a gash in the earth's surface, the glow of hot embers and the wailing of a stricken people. Yet 'hella' is from the Norse *hella*, meaning a cave. It is an awesome gorge. A farmer said, 'I don't know if there's any spot like it, really.'

The Gill is tucked away from the sight of the world. To the Victorian writers, it was 'this Stygian rivulet'. Edmund Bogg thought the name Hell Gill a misnomer, 'if we might judge from the peat-browned unruly torrent that lashes through the tortuous gorge in times of storm.' Leland, an earlier topographer, had heard that 'the bek cawled Hell Gille' was so named because 'it runneth in such a deadly place'.

The final act in the drama is where the water from Hell Gill leaps from a high limestone slab with the verve of Niagara, white as milk, seething as it encounters the dark rocks far below. Behind the grey curtain of water is an outstanding section through the Yoredale series of rocks. The Force—to use an old Norse word—is seen by motorists and also rail passengers at Aisgill, the summit length of the Settle-Carlisle railway. This border country has long been noted for the quality of its Swaledale sheep. Chris Alderson, a local farmer, told me that the area is good for sheep, with both heather and mosscrops. His sheep grazed Hugh's Seat, an eminence named after Hugh de Morville. This local landowner was one of the four knights implicated in the murder of Thomas à Becket.

As I strode towards Hell Gill Farm, the fields were verdant and the fabric of the house was in good condition, having been renovated by a couple from Blackpool. I donned wellies and waded into the mouth of the Hell Gill itself, carefully negotiating waterfalls and inching my way around quite deep pools. Rounded pebbles could be viewed through the gin-clear water as though through a sheet of plate glass. It was chilly within the gorge, but looking up I saw the lush greenery of sunlit leaves. Trees cluster on either side of Hell Gill.

In a spell of dry weather, a novel experience awaits the walker who traverses Hell Gill, for normally, there is a strong flow of water, the beck draining the eastern side of the far-flung Mallerstang Common. Swimming trunks and plimsolls are the recommended wear, there being a compulsory swim on at least three occasions. A ladder was formerly kept in the locality to be used by the shepherd recovering the bodies of sheep. Once a horse fell in and was drowned. The carcase had to be cut into sections for lifting to the surface and subsequent burial.

The bridge spanning Hell Gill forms part of an ancient route used for centuries. It is said that the Romans came this way. Lady Anne, in the seventeenth century, followed the fell route from Cotterdale to her castle in Mallerstang, her horse-drawn carriage being without springs. At the time of Brough Hill horse fair, an autumnal event, local people used to erect stalls near the bridge and sell wares to travellers. Did the highwayman Dick Turpin leap across the gorge on Black Bess while escaping from the constables of Westmorland? That is the tradition. Turpin's Leap is one of the local features.

It has been suggested that this wild countryside was away from the normal haunts of Dick Turpin and that the local villain, Will Nevison, might have been implicated. The Very Rev T. W. Ingram Cleasby, whose family had territorial links with the area going back to the eighteenth century, told me the feat is quite possible: the father of the late Mr George Atkinson, who formerly farmed at Aisgill, told him that he had jumped across the gorge himself as a youth. 'I have no wish to emulate his feat,' the Dean added.

To walk on the airy ridge above Mallerstang on a clear day is a joyful experience; it befell Bob Swallow, Stan Field and myself one October, when the bracken fronds had died back to stain the fellsides with a coppery hue. We used two cars, parking one near The Moorcock and the other at Kirkby Stephen railway station. The footpath led by Blades Farm to join the High Way near where High Dyke Farm, at 1,400 feet, once combined farming with inn-keeping and catered for travellers through this wild country. The farm is now a ruin—for the trade shifted to the new routes that were developed on lower ground—but enough remains to hint at its former importance.

The walker who reaches Mallerstang Edge finds sharp-edge gritstone and a breath-taking downward sweep to the dale itself. (I have driven up Mallerstang when a strong wind was battering the Edge and blowing the becks back on themselves, so that spray was rising like smoke). From the heights, a southward view takes in Whernside and Ingleborough; Wild Boar Fell blocks out half the sky to the west. The fells gradually lose height as the Eden Valley is neared. Soon, the upper valley of the Swale is revealed. So clear were the conditions when last I walked the Edge that I could pick out the tiny white form of Tan Hill Inn.

I never drive into Mallerstang without thinking of an indomitable little dalesman, Jossie Atkinson, who lived alone on Cumpstone Hill, a farm perched on the side of the valley close to Lady Anne's route. When I last saw him, he was 'turned eighty-six' and hopped about on 'my pot foot'. I had crossed open fields and climbed a hillside to reach him, so—as he conceded—'I'm nut likely to be knocked down bi a car.' If he had a special skill, it was drystone walling. Many of the old boundaries of Mallerstang had the mark of Jossie Atkinson upon them. Otherwise, he was a small-time farmer. He invited me into his kitchen-cum-living room, where I saw a huge fireplace incorporating an oven and wash-boiler, a flagged floor with pegged rug and a large deal table. The whole room was worthy of being transferred without change to a folk museum.

He recalled a time when a housekeeper used the oven to cook beef, Christmas loaf and pasties of various kinds, fuelling it with peat gathered from the fell, augmented with a little coal. I saw a reckon, from which a copper kettle was suspended. Beyond lay the dark opening of the chimney. Jossie confessed it had not been cleaned out for years. He used to climb on the house top and drop down the chimney a sled rope with a big stone as a weight. He then tied to the rope a sack filled with bracken. When the bottom of the chimney had been blocked off, the sack was pulled up and down a number of times, displacing the soot.

Jossie had taken up residence at the farm in 1930, which was not a good time because of industrial depression and low prices. Sheep taken to market then 'browt nowt'. He had memories of trudging around the fells in hot weather looking for sheep that had been 'struck wi' maggots'. He did not think that farmers bothered as much with their sheep today.

'In the old days they were forever "looking" their sheep. They could nearly always find summat wrang!' Clogs were commonly worn and were ideal for 'turning snow broth' (at the time of the thaw), though if the snow was crisp the clog-irons tended to collect it and 'you'd be walking along on lumps of hard-packed snow.' Jossie used to recall with joy the time of pig-killing—more precisely, the time when home-fed and home-cured pork was being eaten and 'fat fair dribbled from t'sides of thee mouth'. In days when people worked hard physically, and no one knew much about calories, pigs were bred fat. 'I killed one here when t'last war was on and I rendered down 28 pound o' fat. By gum, it come in useful did that. We were rationed for lard then. When you fried, you could get a potful of fat oot o' t'frying pan.'

Jossie used to collect his peat with a horse-drawn coup (a sled holding a wooden-sided box). He went to a hill-end pit in Cotterdale for coal with a horse and cart. The cart took eight hundredweight, and the cost of a load of coal was about 3s 6d. 'Cotterdale coal was small. You poured it onto a hot peat fire and let it cake. Then you had a stab at it wi' a poker!'

I was fascinated to see that Jossie's farmhouse had a 'beef baulk': it was the second one I had seen. The ceiling immediately against the fire was cut away and a box-like device made to extend it into the room above. Up here, a lid could be lifted and beef—or any other meat—could be placed to dry out slowly under the influence of heat from the fire. Jossie explained that the meat was salted for long-keeping. 'There were no butchers round here then, you know.' He himself did some 'butching' just after the 1914–18 war and I was told about a Grisedale man who each November liberally fed about 100 wether hoggs and then 'butched' six every Monday morning. The meat was taken to Hawes.

Then Jossie got on to the subject of cures for cattle. I'd asked about a cupboard set in the wall. Did he keep his salt there, to keep dry?

'We kept all sorts o' bits o' things, maybe bottles of cow medicine. I used to doctor my own cows, not send for t'vet.

If I had a cow that had calved but didn't cleanse, or part
with its placenta, within five or six hours, I'd wait until it
had been calved 24 hours and then get a pint o' cream and a
tablespoonful of salt petre. I'd mix 'em together and put the
mixture into an old cow horn and give the stuff to the cow
through the mouth. In an hour or two, you'd see the
cleansing come. If it didn't just shift it, you had to give it
another dose, 12 hours after. But it nearly always worked
first time . . .'

Months later, I told the Hodgsons of New Ing Farm about
Jossie's remedy. And months after that, a farmer visited
them, who was anxious because he had a cow that had not
'cleansed' properly. He was told about the cream-and-salt
petre cure and determined to use it. He did not mention it to
his son, for fear of being ridiculed. But it worked, and then
he admitted what he had done.

* * *

I usually approached Teesdale from Brough, on a road that
soon shrugs off the company of walls. From it I admired the
long, lean outline of Mickle Fell, which formerly was the
highest fell in Yorkshire. Then I would see a ridge-to-ridge
fitted carpet of heather. Near Middleton-in-Teesdale, I
looked for the start of the cul-de-sac road through Strath-
more terrain to Holwick which, prior to the 1974 boundary
review, was Yorkshire's most northerly settlement. Now I
could give my attention to upper Teesdale, where lime-
washed farms and cottages stood out, dreamy white,
against lush meadows, with the tawny fells providing an
impressive background to every view.

On my latest visit, the sun shone unhindered by cloud
after a summer which, in the upper dale, had been generally 'cold and black'. Farmers in this area have their wits
tested by the climatic excesses—though very hot days are
rare. It is an area of low temperatures, high rainfall and
much snow in winter. In some years, the growing season
seems to be little more than a good-natured wink between the rigours of spring and autumn. A minus three

Centigrade temperature was recorded at Cow Green on a Saturday evening—in August!

The arctic-alpine flora of the dalehead is world famous. Botanists also rejoice when they see some of Teesdale's herby meadows—a rarity in themselves on the Pennines, now that even fell farmers have taken up silage-making as a way of securing reasonable crops of grass in uneasy weather. The dale farmers manage their 'inby' lands and turn out their sheep to summer on the 'outby' areas, or fells, where the land is elevated and unimproved. The bonnie heather blooms on dry ridges and the hollows are lagged by sphagnum. Between 1600 and about 1900, a dual economy was practised, with many of the men engaging in mining —some staying away from home on weekdays while the women and young people cared for the farm.

Teesdale north of the river is part of the farflung Raby Estate. Most of the farms are constructed of limestone, with some whinstone; the walls may be up to two feet thick, but—the stone being porous—they tend to be damp. Part of the enchantment of the area is the architectural variety, yet unity is preserved by the white walls. Great pride is taken by the estate and tenants in ensuring that those walls are regularly whitewashed. When I mentioned to one farmer the whitewashed farms, including his own, he recalled the time when cob lime was burnt in one of the field kilns that could be seen from the farm. The cob lime, locally called 'clot lime', had to be 'slaked' before being used.

The Tees is a spectacular river, even though the prospect of the dalehead was dramatically changed, and the vagaries of the river somewhat subdued, by the creation of a large, river-regulating dam at Cow Green. Cauldron Snout is where the infant river flows down a natural staircase formed of whin sill. At High Force, a river headstrong with water it has collected from as far away as Cross Fell, thunders over an eroded cliff of whin sill into a dark pool. The time to visit High Force is during a sudden thaw, as snow melts on the high Pennines. Then a single mighty fall on what used to be the Yorkshire side of the river becomes two falls as the Durham channel fills and overflows, leaving a middle rock which has also been known to vanish under white water.

Sunny conditions lull visitors into a belief that all is well with the world. High Force lies under a blue summer sky. Then thunderstorms bombard Cross Fell. There is an ominous hush. Suddenly, and still in sunshine, the Tees breaks into flood. Even local people talk in hushed tones about the Tees 'roll'—a wall of water ranging in height from about three to six feet and extending across the channel, moving at a speed of from four to five miles an hour. At floodtime, the thunder and boom of High Force can be heard nearly a mile away.

Much further down the river, at Low Falls, a rolling mass of water has been just a few inches from the bottom of the suspension bridge—an old bridge, famous among engineers. Some 30 years ago, salmon were seen here, but the fish were eventually unable to negotiate the grossly polluted reaches of the Tees near its mouth. Now that the river has been cleaned up, salmon are returning: they have been seen at Barnard Castle. It is a hopeful note on which to end.

Chapter 17

Up t'Ginnel

We moved our *Dalesman* office from Fellside to the buildings 'up t'ginnel'. Eddie Gower, the advertising manager, had been operating from home, The Beeches, at the head of the village. Eddie, who had previously lived in Baildon, came to us with the required knowledge of advertising and also as an artist who in succeeding years covered several thousand pieces of white card with fine drawings in Indian ink. The drawings ranged from impressions of stately homes to 'heads and shoulders' of Swaledale sheep or red fox.

An authentic Dales garden was established by Alan Burtt. He was a Quaker friend of the Scotts who came to live in the district and who, for many years, contributed to the success of the little company, as bookkeeper, writer of a series of natural history articles, indexer, and proof-reader. During his time, the magazine was virtually free of typographical and grammatical errors, as many readers pointed out when writing to us with renewals of their subscriptions. He moved to a quiet house near the Hambleton Hills.

The garden made by Alan Burtt had an authentic appearance because he used limestone from Ingleborough, trees from a nursery near Tebay and an instant lawn from Newby Moor, a tract of open ground beside the A65 known to car-trippers from the towns as 'Clapham Common'. One of our staff had a right to lift turf.

In due course, we were joined by Dennis Bullock, a native of the district who was to take charge of the financial aspects of the firm. Many earlier decisions had been taken on impulse—Harry Scott once fixed the price of a book while travelling to the printer with the final proofs, and the price turned out to be less than the cost of production! In succeeding years, Dennis augmented the spirit of idealism with the vital 'balancing of the books'. He had not been with us long when Harry Scott said, wrily, 'If you go on like this, we might actually make a profit . . .' The fact that Dennis is still in charge of finances, and the company is solvent, reflects his skill with costings.

To what Harry Scott liked to think of as 'the Dalesman family' came Tony Jefferies, to be in charge of sales, and David Joy, a member of an old Upper Wharfedale family, who spent many years developing a *Dalesman* book list. It contains several hundred worthy titles at any given moment.

By great good fortune, one of the vicars of Clapham was elderly and somewhat lame. The vicarage was huge, the garden vast and the vicar's inclination to tend flowers and vegetables slight, so we were able to purchase from the Ecclesiastical Commissioners a tract of garden and a building in which old-time vicars stabled their horses. For a time, our part of the garden was approached through a door driven into the wall of the office kitchen. The editorial department having been transferred to the former stable block, one hoped for fine weather when carrying valuable artwork or documents to and from the main office, on a grit path near rose beds and other faded glories of the vicarage garden.

The roof of the stable block was in a shocking state. It would have been easy to replace it with grey tiles, but it was decreed that the flags would be removed, the building retimbered and the flags returned, a protracted and expensive job. The grand plan allowed for the upper room to be a store for books and the ground floor to be editorial offices, but after a while there were ominous creaks as the books reminded us that paper weighs heavily. So the roles were reversed, and editorially we went up in the world—after watching a typical Dales craftsman knock spaces in the masonry to accommodate windows. He did this with only the merest glance at the plan, and by 't'rack o' t'eye'. Not until a careless pheasant flew through a pane of glass in recent times did we have any trouble with the windows so skilfully created. And you could hardly blame the craftsman for the navigational error of a wild bird.

We had a small kitchen, and newcomers to the staff tried to cook themselves five-course meals until they acknowledged that facilities were too slight. They settled for beans on toast. At one time fish and chips might be purchased at a side door of the New Inn—a door leading directly into the kitchen—but I did not avail myself of this. I could remember when Don Mills toured the villages in the evening with a large van in which he cooked fish and chips while the customers waited. The Scotts, when visiting us from their retirement home, were fond of recalling the old days, and it was Dorothy who once mentioned the mobile fishery of Don Mills. On winter nights, with the prevailing wind from the south-west, the vinegary tang could be detected over a third of the village. Lighting was by courtesy of a paraffin lamp. A small metal chimney connected to the range sent vapour into the frosty air. Don's fish and chips tasted especially good when eaten from paper on a frosty night.

Dorothy recalled another fish and chip shop, too, opened by the Towlers who were also the butchers. I patronised the place at lunchtime on its first day and Mrs Towler, knowing of my connection with journalism, suggested that I might send off a paragraph about her enterprise to the *Craven Herald*. This I did. The following week, a doleful Mrs Towler informed me that among those who had read the piece was the local sanitary inspector, who had sent an emissary to her premises. So many conditions had been laid down that she had decided to stop cooking fish and chips.

In January, 1960, the house at Austwick having become too small for the Mitchell family, we moved to Settle. I usually drove home for lunch, and one day, as I arrived, my wife hurried to the door, looking somewhat flustered, and announced that there were visitors in the front room—J. B.

Priestley and his wife Jacquetta. They had been given my
name and address by a friend who was on the staff of *Life
International* and who had commissioned JB to write an
article about the Dales. The best known Yorkshireman was
then 70 years of age. His stocky form rested in our most
comfortable chair; I recognised instantly that sagging face,
the steady eyes set under beetling brows and the firm
mouth into which a briar pipe fitted as of right. He had
courteously refrained from smoking. With his pipe in full
blast, my eyes would have been watering.

JB apologised for arriving just before lunch—and on
baking day. Could I recommend a café where he and his
wife might have a meal? I mentioned the hotels, but he
wanted 'nowhere posh'. I directed him to a café and afterwards he reported that the meal was 'not too bad'. In fact, it
was a distinctly old-fashioned sort of café, right down to the
elderly waitress in print pinafore who shouted down a hoist
for 'sausage and chips' and other products of deep-frying.
When my sister and wife called a day or two later they had a
snack that included a sweet described on the menu as
'plumbs and custard'.

Jacquetta went off to Victoria Cave, taking the car, which
she proposed to leave at the roadside. Somehow, JB managed to squeeze into my tiny car for a crossing of Buckhaw
Brow to the *Dalesman* office at Clapham. There, Harry Scott
and JB settled back for a chat, stoked up their pipes and
talked away the afternoon. When I rejoined them, visibility
was down to a few yards. The article written by JB mentioned his visit and commented on the fact that the ladies
who were packing the latest issue of *The Dalesman* sang and
chattered the whole time.

I met JB in his favourite Wensleydale. It was a bright
morning, with a curlew-busy sky. He was staying at the
Rose and Crown in Bainbridge, just across the road from
Dick Chapman and just across the dale from Marie Hartley
and Joan Ingilby. These three were his favourite dalesfolk.
For a time I stood outside the hotel, listening to the patter of
his typewriter keys and watching the occasional wraith of

tobacco smoke drift from the open window. We then conversed in a series of shouts, he from the open window, myself at ground level. It was arranged that we would meet at Muker for a chat, and then he allowed me to photograph him, close up, with a variety of facial expressions. He had donned his old blue beret.

It was JB who had introduced our first issue of *The Yorkshire Dalesman* in 1939. In a brief note, he recalled his demobilisation from the army in the spring of 1919 (just twenty years previously) and his first writing job, a short series dealing with a walking tour in the Dales. He tramped through Upper Wharfedale and crossed to Wensleydale, mentioning 'the sunlight that set all the dewdrops glittering about my path'.

In March, 1964, *The Dalesman* attained its 25th birthday, with no special fuss but with a monthly circulation of 60,000 and a readership that was not far short of half a million. It was easily the top magazine in the country with regard to sales. We were quietly gratified by the many friendly letters from readers testifying to the magazine's appeal. It was Yorkshire through and through and unashamedly old-fashioned. When a visitor to our offices spoke loftily of *The Dalesman* as being 'a magazine for amateurs, produced by amateurs', Harry Scott took it as a compliment! Our readers were one big and usually happy family. Their many letters ensured that our pages would be tinged by nostalgia; their amusing tales of Yorkshire folk, scattered about each issue, were greeted with delight, even though a traditional tale might appear at regular intervals. Our readers were loyal, as reflected by the steadiness of our sales, at home and abroad. A reader who on retirement journeyed round the world, told us she had a feeling that wherever she might be there would be a copy of *The Dalesman* no more than a mile away!

In 1964, Harry Scott was nudging sixty, but at Clapham the staff still numbered only 16. In 1951, we had taken over *Cumbria*, a regional magazine for the Lake District that was founded and being published by the Youth Hostels'

Association. The circulation was 1,000 per month. Editing
Cumbria had been my task from the start; I now had the
joyful experience, usually once a week, of venturing into a
considerable tract of the North Country, from Solway to the
Humber and from the Tees to the Hodder, in Bowland. The
editorial office work must be maintained and I also managed to fit in the editorial aspects of book publishing. It was
a time in my life when I became aware that my fingers were
turning upwards at the ends through over-use of a
typewriter keyboard.

The Dalesman joined the Audit Bureau of Circulations in
1950, when the average net sale per issue was 19,423. The
price rose to one shilling, and now readers reminded us
frequently of the threepence charged during the war. We
gently pointed out that for a shilling we provided 86 pages,
some of which carried colour. In 1960, all our printing was
transferred to Messrs Atkinson and Pollitt, of Kendal. A
welcome visitor to the office was Harry Firth, the works
manager, who became a personal friend and maintained a
high standard of printing. The most anxious moments were
when he experimented, at our request, with coated zinc
blocks for the cover picture. The first of the set began to
wear badly as the 65,000 printing run developed. Harry
Firth kept in touch with us at half-hourly intervals until,
with much nursing, a picture of a sort had been
reproduced.

Dick Clarke, a retired railway signalman who lived in
Clapham, was delighted to be asked to help at the *Dalesman*
offices. His routine was not prescribed: he was told just to
keep himself busy. I remembered Dick as the man who
daily, for 19 years, had cycled to and from the signal box at
Helwith Bridge. His wife, Sally, insisted on him wearing
plenty of flannel. In summer he sweated so freely his face
was the colour of the rising sun. Sally ignored the teasing of
local people: her Dick must not get a chill. Dick's favourite
railway story was of the day part of an ammunition train
broke loose at Blea Moor and the wagons, with their
dangerous cargo, rattled merrily down the wrong track

towards Settle. As Dick told it, he remained on duty and saw those wagons careering out of control just a few yards away. As other railwaymen recalled, Dick was out of the box and away up the field as soon as he realised the danger. And who could blame him?

This good-natured man gave scores of his paintings to the annual church sale. To meet the demand, he devised a method of mass production. Once, visiting his house at the height of pre-sale production, I watched with amazement as he laid half a dozen blank sheets of paper along the edge of a table, and then moved along the line several times, applying various washes—first blue, for the sky: all six skies, one after another; then grey for the church tower and green for the croft in the foreground. He carefully spread the wet pictures on newspaper to dry—and reached for another batch of blank paper!

Financially, *The Dalesman* just about broke even. Harry had wrily observed, 'If we're not careful, we'll make a profit!' The cover price of a shilling was scarcely enough to pay for printing and to cover overheads. We gave Eddie Gower all support in obtaining advertisements. Hotels and boarding houses found our appeal considerable; small-time businesses and craftsmen could advertise in our 'Yorkshire Shop Window—*The Dalesman*'s bargain department store.' We charged ninepence a word for classified advertising, which accounted for about half of the advertising space. We raised by classifieds as much money as we did with display advertising at £55 a page. A wartime advertisement was novel in that the printer, Harold Lambert, left a quarter of a page blank and we attached to it gummed stickers for a brand of tea. It was the first colour advertisement we carried.

The 'Personal' section sometimes offended the more prudish readers, though there was nothing salacious. When I addressed members of the Leeds Chamber of Trade, the man who introduced me mischievously mentioned the interest he found in reading the 'Personal' column, and quoted one or two examples. Fortunately, I recalled—and used in response—our only pornographic joke. When two Dales farmers met at the auction mart, one remarked, 'What about all this pornography?' The other replied, 'Don't know, lad. I haven't getten a pornograph.'

Humour was an essential element in making up *The Dalesman*. It was evident for some years in a series of amusing poems in dialect about a lad called 'Young Fred'. He was created and sustained by a West Riding man, Will Clemence, and caused much hilarity, except to those parents who wanted their children to 'talk proper' and found that, having read 'Young Fred', they were using Yorkshirisms like 'flipping heck'. When Will Clemence shuffled off this mortal coil, his place was taken by Rowland Lindup, another man born and reared in the West Riding. His creation, 'Old Amos', continues to this day. Rowland came in to see me and produced a miniature tape recorder of which he was very proud. He wanted to interview me, and I managed to switch roles and interview him about Amos, a Yorkshire Peter Pan in the sense that he did not grow older.

Rowland recalled that, in the early 1950s, he was visited by the representative of a group called the Kingstown Artists, for whom he drew some cartoons. These were passed to Harry Scott, who sent a letter asking for further ideas. A consequence was the 'Old Amos' series, commissioned by Harry Scott and continuing because 'no one has told me to stop'. I was told by Rowland that the name came from an old man he knew. 'I thought it was an unusual name, but probably typical of Yorkshire. Nobody is called Amos today.' Of the several drawings he made of Amos, he retained one with a long, white beard, 'which saves me drawing a collar and tie.'

One month, Amos said, 'Ah reckon it is a waste o' brass to buy an alarm clock for a chap 'at's med up his mind to stay in bed.' Another month: 'Middle age is when it taks twice as long to rest an' 'alf as long to git tired.' He was shown sitting in a pub, with a pint at his side, remarking, 'What tha wants for working is a cast-iron back wi' a hinge on it.' Mentioning a friend who was retired and had nothing to do, Amos said, 'He were like a woodpecker wi' out a tree.'

The old sage actually helped me to transform the animosity of a well-known Yorkshireman into friendship. I was reading proofs of *The Dalesman* and came across Amos's remark that 't'best way to impress folk is to let em impress you'. That evening, at a dinner, I was sitting beside a guest who, for some reason unknown to me, made some unkind remarks about the magazine. I listened to all he had to say. I mentioned his great abilities and spoke highly of work he had done. At the end of the evening, *The Dalesman* had another enthusiastic supporter, and such he has remained over many years.

Loyalty to the magazine has been demonstrated by many contributors, and is evident among those whose work first appeared in our pages. I had been familiar with the name Dr Arthur Raistrick since my boyhood days, for the *Craven Herald* reported on his archaeological activities. He had a distinguished academic career in Newcastle, and his researches in the Dales were presented immaculately in papers and books. His contributions to *The Dalesman* distinguished early issues and his *Malham and Malham Moor*, illustrated in colour by another Quaker, Constance Pearson, has become a classic.

From time to time I called to see Arthur Raistrick at his Dales home, an early example of the old barn converted into living accommodation. If it was baking day, his wife Elizabeth would invite me into the kitchen to sample freshly-baked scones, with knobs of butter, and coffee to follow. After conversing with Arthur, I would leave Home Croft at Linton with the stimulus of fresh ideas.

We discussed the possible origin of the name Wild Boar Fell, the hill dominating Mallerstang, which I felt was more likely to have been the haunts of wolves than of swine. Once, when I arrived stating that I had just had a bad attack of nostalgia, recalling a brass band playing the hymn tune 'Deep Harmony' in Skipton High Street on a Saturday afternoon in the 1930s, he casually mentioned that when he was a boy, living in the Aire Valley, he had attended a practice of a choir conducted by the hymn's composer, Handel Parker—a practice at which the new hymn tune was being sung! Arthur has celebrated his 90th birthday, and I invited a few close friends to contribute congratulatory messages to *The Dalesman*. These moved him deeply.

We published the first article to be penned by William Foggitt, who became famous as the Weather Man. I arrived at his home, South Villa, Thirsk, on the same day as *The Methodist Recorder*, and he had already read a good deal of it. Methodism and the Foggitts have been closely connected since 1809. William, who is a local preacher, told me, 'When I started preaching in 1938, I was always expecting people to come up to me afterwards to discuss the sermon. Now, whatever I say, it will always be: "Hello, Bill. What's the weather going to do then?"'

He reminded me, as we talked, that it was in 1949 we published his article on Britain's rare orchids. He told me that his interest in the weather was stimulated by seeing the total eclipse of the sun on June 29, 1927. He wrote some notes about it, and his father told him to keep it up. 'Write something every day and you'll get a nice diary at Christmas.' He received a 1928 diary, which he has still got. 'It was an interesting year. There was a good summer. King George V was very ill. Thomas Hardy died. I used to keep an obituary list.'

When I asked William Foggitt about his forecasts, he immediately distinguished between daily forecasts and long-range forecasts. Each morning, on rising, he scans the barometer. 'Locally, you can't beat it for accuracy . . .' He takes note of the wind's speed and direction. In the absence of a weather vane at his home, he reaches for binoculars and consults the vane on the church tower at Thirsk. He records the rainfall and looks around for any special natural signs—midges, for instance. Ever ready to admit any shortcomings, he said he had only recently become aware of the difference between midges and gnats.

He speaks well of television forecasters and says they are more often right than wrong. Yet he recalls when a journalist rang him in the middle of January, during a severe spell of weather, and asked how long the cold snap would last. William consulted the barometer, which was falling. He had just noticed that moles were starting up, so he said, 'Oh, there'll be a thaw.' 'When?' asked the journalist. William thought he would not rush matters and said, 'Thursday.' On that day the weathermen brought into service a new computer and they forecast a blizzard. Instead, there was a thaw, as William Foggitt had foretold! His mind is a repository of worthwhile country lore. A journalist working on a brash tabloid newspaper rang him up for some observations about the weather. 'I said, "The cuckoo's silent. That shows it's pretty cold."' Next morning, the headline proclaimed: SILENT CUCKOO TELLS ALL!

Another old friend, William Cowley, contributed farming articles to *The Dalesman* for years and, in one of them, put forward the idea which led to the establishment of the Lyke Wake Walk, a 40-mile slog across the North York Moors, from Osmotherley to the sea at Ravenscar. After a varied career, including years spent in the Indian Civil Service, he bought a 21-acre small-holding at Over Silton and eventually moved to Potto Hill, a 46-acre farm on the clayey Cleveland Plain. The name of the Walk came from an old Cleveland funeral dirge, and Bill became the Chief Dirger when an organisation was formed and its activities were ritualised.

Charles Graham, who called to see me at the office, was an enthusiastic rock-gardener and an admirer of Reginald Farrer. As I followed what had become the Reginald Farrer Trail through Clapdale, I would stop at the head of the lake on hearing a rustle of vegetation. Sometimes there would be the sound of a hand-saw or the clatter of stones in the gorge. I would then look for Charles Graham, who had set himself the task of rehabilitating the area where Farrer had planted rhododendrons and bamboos. Farrer had noted that in this predominantly limestone area there is, at the head of Ingleborough lake, an outcrop of Silurian slate, with the acidic conditions beloved of rhodies.

Mr Graham—I never called him Charles—heard Geoffrey Smith deliver a Farrer Memorial Lecture in the village and this inspired him to rescue and restore the Farrer rhododendrons after 30 years of neglect. The landowner, Dr John Farrer, was agreeable to the work being done. Mr Graham told him in no uncertain terms that it would be carried out without charge, though he did agree to take some motoring expenses once a year. So he went forth, with saw and axe and fork—'a committee of one'. Knowing of my long-time interest in Reginald Farrer, he called from time to time to report progress. His daily routine was fascinating. An 'early bird', he drove his old blue car over Buckhaw Brow to arrive in the village as early as 6 a.m. The car boot held a mass of assorted objects, from string to a spade. Parking his car near the Estate office, he made a selection from the implements and sauntered into the woods. He had a snack meal of cheese and dry bread. By 2-30, he was back in the village, ready to return home, where he ate some boiled onions and slipped into bed for a couple of hours to rest and read.

As an octogenarian, he amazed us with his energy and sense of purpose. He felled unwanted sycamores, hazels and birches. He developed the technique of using a rope to swing along the sides of the gorge, with saw and axe, clinging to any part where he wished to remove unwanted trees. The branches and sections of trunk fell into the beck and, having a tidy mind, he then descended to the level of the beck to remove the tangle.

He found seedlings that had lodged in moss or between tree roots. Some were struggling in crannies in the outcropping slate. They were transported to Giggleswick and given nursery conditions at his home until he judged it wise to return them to the wild. The seedlings grown in pans were transferred to peat beds. In 1983, some of his reintroduced plants were four feet high and in flower.

One day, while he was working at Clapham, Charles

Graham was injured when a tree rolled onto him. He walked back to the village using the shaft of his fork as a crutch and was laid up at home for six weeks. He then returned to his self-imposed task. The accident was never mentioned again.

Chapter 18

A Seaside Home

When Harry Scott retired from full-time work at *The Dalesman*, he and his wife moved to Grange-over-Sands. At first, he returned each Friday, to look at any mail, to gather up review copies of books, to go out for a meal and to chat with Dennis Bullock about the financial aspects of the company. A scheme was devised by which four of us—Dennis, Tony Jefferies, David Joy and myself—would purchase shares and continue the enterprise without radical change.

At his new detached home in Charney Road, Harry was delighted if we called. We would sip coffee and chat about things that gave him pleasure, not mentioning our concern about the steeply rising cost of paper. We beheld from the window the gleaming sands of Morecambe Bay and did not broach matters concerning the cost of printing books. In the days when Harry Scott had negotiated with a printer, the price rise would be two per cent or five per cent. Now much stronger inflationary pressures were affecting British publishing as a whole. Harry, mercifully, knew little or nothing about them in his retirement home on the sunny side of the Bay.

We were shown the goldfish pond, the revolving summer house or the latest acquisitions for the garden. He was generous in taking us out for meals, and there were no prizes for guessing that he would choose trout. Such meals were enjoyed at one of the hotels where an Edwardian flavour lingered on. Then it was back to work. A new printer, Alf Smith of Bradford, had up-to-date lithographic presses. I would smile at the recollection of experiments

Harry had conducted into the production of cheaper printing blocks. There was the 'coated zinc' phase, which played
havoc with our nervous systems when a long run, over
60,000 copies, was in progress. I kept in hourly touch with
the anxious printer who had reported deterioration of the
yellow or the red block. Ironically, at that time our cover
artist had portrayed a new house being shown by the proud
builder to a dubious couple. The lady was looking with
some concern at a corner of the building where a piece of
stiffened paper with a brick pattern printed upon it was
hanging loose!

Harry did not care much for lithography. He kept a large
selection of badly printed lithographic booklets and magazines in the bottom drawer of his desk. Should the possibility of ourselves using lithography be raised, he would take
a grim example from the heap in the drawer and toss it
towards us. In other respects, he was keen on innovation
and had, indeed, used colour pictures in the magazine
when colour was a novelty. Modern methods of making
'separations', using laser beam, would have fascinated
him. He worried steadily about the cost of blocks and
dreamed of being the designer of a small box into which a
colour picture would be placed, a lever drawn—and the set
of blocks collected from a drawer at the bottom end of the
machine!

He had a happy retirement. His days were spent quietly,
reading his books. Friends took the Scotts for runs into the
Lake District, and he enjoyed returning with a memento
—a book, a pot of local jam or a car boot filled with logs for
the winter fire.

He found pleasure in the company of his children and
grandchildren, and he and Dorothy were invited to each
pre-Christmas party at Clapham. I was with him at Grange
on the day before he died. He listened with interest to
up-to-date information about the affairs at The Dalesman.
Death came suddenly, swiftly, from a massive heart attack
during a morning walk.

We attended the cremation at Lancaster. I had forgotten

to don a black tie and one of our group arranged for me to call at a friend's house on the way to Lancaster. A black tie was borrowed. Later, I realised that it would have impressed few who attended, for Quakers do not put great store on outward show. I heard from a Clapham mother about the time her family and the Scotts went for a day's trip to Lakeland; they crossed Windermere by the ferry. As the boat ran up the shingly beach, the woman's small son asked about the sound. Harry Scott remarked, 'It's only a chaffinch grinding its teeth.' That small boy never forgot about a certain Lakeland chaffinch.

At a simple little ceremony at Clapham, Harry's ashes were placed among the roses in the garden. We assembled in our best clothes as a mark of respect. As Harry's brother-in-law spoke at length about him, rain fell heavily and none of us wished to break ranks to collect umbrellas or raincoats. If the human spirit is indestructible, then Harry would have been chuckling quietly at our plight.

Dorothy Scott lived on until 1987, first at Grange—she moved to a bungalow at the quaintly-named Cat Tree Road—and then at Hexham, where she was near her daughter. The memorial service took place at the Quaker meeting house in Cartmel. On a quiet Saturday, the daughter and her husband placed the ashes near those of Harry in a corner of the *Dalesman* garden.

Chapter 19

Spoken Words

Having bought a tape-recorder, I sallied forth into the Dales. One man became hot-under-the-collar about upland forestry and got dangerously near to swearing as he spoke about the big new conifer plantations. When the interview was over, I wound back some of the tape so that he might hear his own voice. The extract, chosen at random, was his denunciation of forestry. He listened for a couple of minutes and declared, 'I knew I was reight—yon chap agrees with me!'

When I was recording, I competed with the ticking of grandfather clocks, with low-flying aircraft and the barking of dogs. Frequently there were background conversations between other members of the family. When chatting with Kit Calvert at Hawes Creamery, I could scarcely hear his voice for the clattering of milk churns. I dropped the recorder several times and subjected it to extremes of temperature, from the heat of a coal fire in a Swaledale farmhouse to the bitter cold of a moortop tarn where I was attempting some wildlife recording—the trumpeting of whooper swans.

None of the recordings approached the minimum standard laid down by the BBC but the machine served its purpose. I had an 'electric notebook' and could capture not only *what* was said but *how* it was said. Such as the recollections of a dalesman who worked on a big sheep farm: 'My boss would stand and watch and smoke his pipe, and say of one animal: "She'll lamb afore mornin." And she did! He really watched his sheep: how they walked about, what they did. He'd get up at night and go out with a lantern. He lived with them sheep, day and night, through lambing time.' A farmer talked to me about hired help in Wensleydale in 1920: 'I was paying the men 10 bob a week, and the girls got 3s 6d or 4s. They worked all the hours I wanted 'em to work. There was no such thing as being paid for overtime. We all got up at six o'clock, and we finished milking at six at night—seven days a week.'

A farmer in Kingsdale warmed himself beside a fire made of home-cut peat, and told me: 'The top peat was mossy. The farther down you went, the better it was, 'cos it was harder. I was once cuttin' peat at t'depth o' this house when I fun (found) a bit o' silver birch.'

With extracts from several interviews, I could round off a whole topic—such as descriptions of the best room of a farmhouse, known as the parlour or the 'front room'. At a large farmhouse in North Ribblesdale, 'we had two big front rooms. We used them alternately, on a Sunday. It was just to keep them aired, really. Sunday was the only time one of those rooms had a fire in it.' In Swaledale, 'there was a carved sideboard—a large one.' A Wensleydale farm had 'a round Victorian table—a mahogany thing. There was a scratchy horsehair sofa. The paraffin lamp was special and had a red bowl and a pink shade . . .'

One unusual memory that impressed me was of baking bread during the 1914–18 war: 'It was haytime. Mother said to me, "I'm thinking that we're not going to have enough bread to see us through. Will you go home and start baking?" It would be about 7 p.m. I went down to the house, lit the fire and got this huge bowl out. My husband was out in France with the Forces. While the bread was rising, I sat down to write him a letter. I remember putting, "It's now 12 o'clock, and I'm just going to take the last lot of bread out."'

The tape-recorder picked up the authentic voices of women talking about porridge, a staple food at farm and cottage. In Wharfedale, 'we used to live on oatmeal porridge and plenty of black treacle, which was a penny a jar.

We'd get a bucketful of blue [skimmed] milk for a penny, and use it on the porridge.' A North Ribblesdale woman recalled, 'We had a big pan, with a handle, and we put it on the reckon, over an open fire. We'd pour into the pan some skimmed milk. When it was nearly on the boil, we'd scatter oatmeal in. If you put the meal in too fast, you had lumps, called "dog 'eeards"; if you had a fall of soot, you had sooty porridge!'

At a time when people were taking cameras and tape-recorders into distant deserts or jungles, I was searching out the unrecorded treasure of the everyday life of dalesfolk who could recall the last years of long centuries of self-sufficiency. The lambing time of 1917 was remembered for the severity of the weather: 'On the first 18 days of April, there was fresh snow every morning. When you went to look t'sheep, they were at back o' t'dykes, and snow had been blown over 'em. Sometimes, all you saw was a horn sticking out. When you got a sheep clear, there'd been a dead lamb or two lying behind it.' That spring, in Wensleydale, 'if a sheep lay down to lamb, she was frozzen to t'grund. We lost over 100 lambs, and maybe 60 to 70 sheep. They hungered to deeath.'

Mrs Sedgwick, who was born and reared in Cowgill, above Dent, cheerfully tolerated several evenings of tape-recording. There was time to go into every aspect of life in the dale, but I remember in particular her recollection of her brother and the stallion, Premier Prince, which he took round the farms and villages in the season when there were farm mares to be mated. An uncastrated stallion was known as an 'entire'.

When he set off on a Monday morning, he would give his sister (now Mrs Sedgwick) a ride to school. The stallion was a Clydesdale, a bay, and 'oh! he had feet on him; they just clamped down and made the ground ring.' When Dent Fair was held, about Whitsuntide, 'we girls got a new straw hat at Billy Burton's and then we rode in style to the Fair in Dad's horse and trap—wi' sixpence in our pockets.'

A farmer told me of points to consider when buying a horse. 'Look for good legs, good shoulders and breast, sweet head and good eye. I've never liked one wi' a lot o' white in t'eye. Same wi' a woman. A lass wi' a lot o' white in t' eye can be bad-tempered!'

With rumours of closure circulating once again, I toured the villages beside the Settle-Carlisle railway and chatted with some of the men who maintained it. Tales of wild weather were commonplace and graphic. At Dent, the weight of ice had snapped the telephone wires. A ganger said: 'It was like the funeral service—"The Lord giveth, and the Lord taketh away."' In 1947, conditions were so bad at Kirkby Stephen that snow-cutters were seen to hang their coats on the tops of the telephone wires.

A driver told me of snow-ploughing in the area of Dent in the 'big snow' of 1963: 'You went through with a plough and one engine first. Reconnoitring. Then you'd need another engine put on, and you'd build up speed and charge the drift, which could be a 200 to 300 yard dash into four or five feet of snow. By the time you'd gone 100 yards, you'd compacted the snow and were beyond the stage at which the plough would cut it. You just came to a juddering halt. Reverse. Try again, till you got through. It was terrifying, especially in daylight. As the snow got deeper you could hear it scratching on the engine. Then the snow came in—between the floorboards of the cab, into every nook and cranny. It was packed so hard the engine became belly-bound. The wheels began to spin. You could be standing on the footplate, up to your waist in snow. It was awful was that snow plough job.'

I have already mentioned Jossie Atkinson, of Mallerstang. It was a railwayman who told me that his wife had been 'a servant lass wi' Jossie, up at Cumpstone Hill. It was her first time out in service, and she was that homesick she could only think o' going out into Jossie's yard now and again and looking out for t'chimneys of Aisgill Cottages, where she was browt up. When she saw the chimneys, it made her day!'

Some of the dalesfolk I met blithely ignored the tape-recorder as they spoke. Mrs Annie Mason, *née* Pratt, told me of her life when the family lived at Burtersett. Her father, James, was a notable cattle dealer who visited Scotland for more than 60 successive years. Her grandfather, Owd Dickie, had his own special job at haytime, going round the land in a horse-drawn float carrying beer in a barrel. 'He did this as early as 4.30 a.m. in the days when the men were mowing the fields by scythe. Then breakfast would be taken round—we always had our porridge, bacon and eggs hot—and at about half-past ten there was a can of coffee and perhaps cheese and bread. For the main meal, even one that took place outdoors, father insisted on hot food. My mother cured him of it—but only after 30 years! He also wanted a change of plates and wouldn't have his pudding on the plate that had held his meat and potatoes.'

James Pratt's main interest when visiting Scotland was to acquire good cattle, but in the back-end of the year he bought some sheep. They were pure Scotlanders, as the Pratts called them. 'Up to the slopes of Wether Fell they went. We got overstocked with sheep in those days, and so they sent some for wintering to Brimham Rocks, above Nidderdale. I remember one winter when there was a big snow as they were due to come back.' Other farmers' sheep had also to be returned to the home farms. The journey of the Pratts' sheep back to Wensleydale would take several days. 'When they had been two or three days coming, I was sent up to beyond Gayle on horseback with two bundles of hay, one on each side of the horse. I would use this hay to 'tice (entice) the sheep down. I also had some provisions —ham sandwiches and various things—for the men to eat. My mother had been to Liverpool and she had bought a thermos flask, the first we'd seen or known about. She made some coffee, put some rum in it and poured it in the thermos flask. I will always remember going up to Old Dick (Fawcett) and asking him if he would like a drop of coffee. He put the thermos to his lips and, of course,

it was full of very hot coffee. "What the devil's in this?"
he shouted.'

It was vital to keep the sheep walking, hence the use of
hay. Over Fleet Moss from Langstrothdale came animals
belonging to the Pratts and the Fawcetts, each sheep tread-
ing in the footsteps of the one that had gone before. 'We
had no trouble "shedding" off Mr Fawcett's sheep. When
they came to his open gate, they "shed" themselves off. I
got to the bottom of the hill and looked back. I could see a
dark line of sheep all the way down the slope.' After her
father's time, the Fawcetts sent their young sheep to the
Lake District for the winter.

It pleased me occasionally to take my tape-recorder to
some well-known Dales event and to collect interviews
with authentic 'backings'. Such an occasion was a flock-
masters' get-together on the high Pennines. This was the
annual Tan Hill show of Swaledale sheep. 'It's allus t'last
Thursdi i' May,' I was told. My first visit was in fog or mist
(to distinguish between them, I was told to put out my
tongue and taste them). A spring date is preferred, because
after lambing the farmers like a chance to have a 'crack'
about the past winter. Many have not met since the October
tup sales.

Friends had told me of the phenomenon of a vacant moor
suddenly filling up with humanity as the show-time drew
nigh. Farmers are not noted for turning up early, and with
only about ten minutes to go, there was scarcely anyone in
sight. Suddenly, there were Land-Rovers and trailers on
every approach road and the best parking spaces were
being occupied. Farmers were out and about, penning
stock or chatting with friends. I saw families with names
that are truly of the Dales—Alderson and Raine, Harker
and Calvert, Garnett and Blades. I saw oldish men with
sensible, if old-fashioned clothes, and with overcoats
buttoned up to the neck. These men sucked pipes of
tobacco—or strong mints. Younger men favoured bright
anoraks. Most had the obligatory wellingtons.

Visiting the pens that had been set up on the moor, close

to the famous inn, I asked a farmer about the condition of the sheep after such a grim winter. 'Nay—thou won't be able to tell at this show,' he asserted. 'This lot will have been in t'parlour. It's them sheep out theer'—and he pointed across the misty moor—'that's t'yardstick!' Another batch of sheep arrived. The animals stood exhaling grey vapour into the grey mist. The man I had met shouted to the owner of a newly-arrived group of sheep, 'Dusta want 'em up here?' There was a nod. The farmer turned to the intervening group of visitors and requested them to stand clear with the words, 'Just make a 'ole.'

The judges began work. They took their time. I mentioned this to an old spectator, who said, 'In these parts, they daren't do owt else.' There was a testiness between animals from different flocks. Two tups faced each other, reversed for several yards, and charged, meeting head to head with a thwack.

Now a ringing sound could be heard in the yard behind the inn. The 'Grand Quoit Match' had begun. Two quoits had collided on a square of puddled clay brought in from the moor 'to make the quoits stick'. The tuneful strains of the Middlesmoor and Lofthouse Silver Band could be heard, the notes rousing any dormant echoes on this high Pennine moor.

Tan Hill has always been a special place to lovers of the Dales. Many a Dales family warmed itself beside a fire of peat and Tan Hill coal. The coal was 'grand shiny stuff', full of gas that hissed and spluttered in the grate. Combined with the peat, it gave an almost savage heat to many a farm and cottage. Matthew Cherry, Bill Alderson (who died in 1988) and Willie Hunter, of Swaledale, told me of local sources of coal—those thin, hard seams occurring in the Yoredale Series of rocks, high on the fells. Another source, in Ivelet, yielded 'bad-burning stuff'. From Stockdale Pit came 'small stuff that didn't cake. It was all right for a smithy fire, for it didn't stick to iron.' Several old pits and mines were re-opened during the 1926 General Strike, when no coal was being consigned to the Dales. Tan Hill's workforce was augmented, and queues developed, customers collecting their supplies by horse and cart.

Harkers, Rukins and Sinclairs were the last families to work the drift-mine that lay some 50 yards from the road between West Stonesdale and Tan Hill Inn. The coal formed a cake; under heat, the pieces ran together. The drift was very wet and well-timbered. The miners had a long walk from their homes and, once underground, they worked by candlelight, the candles being attached to the walls of the mine by knobs of clay. In winter, they scarcely ever saw the sun.

Chapter 20

After Forty Years

Susan Pape, of Yorkshire Television, made an appointment to visit *The Dalesman*. It was the cautious approach, perfected by TV researchers, who usually have a precise idea in mind but would first like to ensure that the people involved have no utterly undesirable attributes—nor the name of a rival Channel tattooed on their cheeks!

The Dalesman had long been associated with what was to become known as 'the media'. In the 1930s Harry Scott wrote extensively about the 'wireless' and made the occasional wartime broadcast from Leeds. My own radio debut, umpteen years ago, was in one programme of a short-lived radio series called *Country Window*, produced by Tom Waldren, who took several of us countryfolk into a Manchester pub and—when he thought we had 'mellowed'—brought us back to a poky studio in a building overlooking Piccadilly, where we were to have an animated conversation. We did—with vowels somewhat slurred.

Now and again, a BBC radio team from Manchester came to see us, to hear a few country tales. Bertha Lonsdale was among them. It was the pre-tape area and equipment was cumbersome. James Gregson, who had been head of drama in the North Region for the BBC, was living at Grassington. His much-loved wife had died, he had no radio work in prospect and was delighted when I suggested he write a series of autobiographical articles for *The Dalesman*.

In a long and varied career in public, James had had more ups and downs than a lift attendant. He had also had a large share of bad luck. In 1939, he was commanding the attention of the BBC, with 11 engagements in prospect. When war broke out, he was promptly forgotten by the broadcasters. 'For the first 12 months of the war, I was making about £3 10s a week sneck-lifting (collecting industrial insurance), and in the second year of the war I was a labourer in a chemical works.' Then the BBC sent for him and asked him to work on *Radio Newsreel* at £640 a year.

After the war, he was back in the north, and for three years was an outstanding regional head of drama. James Gregson was 'Yorkshire through and through'. I shall never forget him describing a man he once knew as 'so bow-legged, he couldn't stop a pig in a ginnel'. For his thriller-serial *Dead Reckoning*—probably the first of the genre ever to go on the air—he spent two hours searching for the noise of a safe door being opened. It took three actors, a peggy-tub on a cushion, a squeaky music stand and a vest-pocket Kodak camera to create an effect that lasted less than ten seconds.

The inquiry by Yorkshire Television prompted thoughts of the chilly day on Holme Moss in 1951 when I attended the opening of the first TV transmitter mast in the North —and marvelled that such a tall structure should rest on a large ball bearing, a rigid form being unsuited to the wild Pennine uplands.

An outstanding television film, in scintillating black-and-white, was Stanley Williamson's *Sheep in High Pastures*—if I recall the title aright—an account of a year's work at Rainscar, one of the big hill sheep farms of the Dales. John Coates and his family cheerfully tolerated the presence of the BBC film crew when they were carrying out seasonal tasks like lambing, clipping, spaining (separating ewes from lambs), and driving their surplus animals overland to Bentham mart. I recall the day when the flock descended from Thwaite Lane into Clapham and moved grandly on with attendant dogs and film camera.

Granada Television included a short film about *The Dalesman* in its *Down to Earth* series; I took them—as I have taken others—to see Arthur Hodgson and his tame deer at

New Ing Farm. The most memorable moment came when the living room was full of a mass of people and equipment. Arthur was being filmed as he chatted about farming, and Bambi the deer was brought into the house to be included in the action.

Bambi picked her way delicately between the complex equipment until she was near the fireplace. Arthur talked on. Suddenly, Twister (the Dalmatian dog) lifted his head to a position he then held for 30 seconds, during which time he howled—a howl which was maintained at top C. Not only did it shatter the peace, it also shattered the nervous system of the sound engineer, who threw away his headphones. Bambi had trodden on Twister's sore leg!

Douglas Smith included the *Dalesman* collection of photographs in his series of *The Magic Lantern Show*, transmitted from Leeds. The selected pictures were copied on to transparencies and in due course a unit arrived at our offices so that I could give a commentary. It was winter; the most suitable place from the point of view of sound was a storeroom, where the walls were lagged by parcels of books. Crouching over a monitor, which was receiving pictures from a camera in an adjacent room, I felt I was acting out part of a wartime Resistance drama, with a secret transmitter. As ever, I admired the unruffled manner in which TV technicians went about their complex work.

Now it was Yorkshire Television's turn. Its film crews had long been familiar with the Dales, and through the long-running series *Emmerdale Farm*—the exteriors originally filmed at Arncliffe—a Dales way of life was being seen in every part of the land. Susan Pape came, saw and persisted in her inquiries. Ian Macfarlane agreed to be the director, remembering no doubt the film he had made about the Settle-Carlisle line. My principal memory of that venture was at Aisgill, the summit of the famous railway, where Ian—standing with the crew beside the line— persuaded the drivers of passing diesel trains to sound their klaxons by the ruse of miming the action of one of the old-time loco drivers operating a steam whistle.

The *Dalesman* film was screened on January 15, 1988, the day of my 60th birthday and of my retirement from the magazine after 40 years. The film opened with a lonely road, a solitary figure (me!) and a single evocative sound —the call of a curlew. This was not the prolonged trilling of the bird in its nesting territory but a snatch of sound, giving the sequence an authentic Dales flavour. The curlew used in the film had migrated from a sound archive but was in that setting by right of 1,000 generations. What matter if, by November, all self-respecting curlews are on low ground, near the western sea?

The stretch of road would be familiar to those whose pleasure is in following the green lanes of the Pennines. Ian had inquired about a road in a wild setting and so we travelled from Bainbridge towards Semerwater, turning off on the old Roman road heading for Fleet Moss. We had enjoyed bar snacks at the Rose and Crown in Bainbridge—a pub with the obligatory beady-eyed, stuffed trout in glass-fronted cases. I had noticed the absence, on duty, of the old forest horn, and I took the opportunity of talking about crayfish with someone who had caught them by the score.

As we ate, sunlight created a Disney-like fantasy of light around a few dark clouds; when we emerged, to resume filming, Sod's Law was operating and curtains of cloud had been drawn across the sun. This did not seem to worry Brian, the cameraman. What fascinated me was the presence of this little convoy at the start of a route that had been used by man for close on 2,000 years. The camera was set up, the sound-recordist signified he was ready and I walked in that majestic setting, trying to avoid looking directly at the bright eye of the camera. In the film, the voice of Alan Bennett is heard saying complimentary things about my association with *The Dalesman* over 40 years, and music by Johann Hummel—a trumpet voluntary—gives a faintly old-fashioned flavour, appropriate in an area that once prided itself on the number and quality of its brass bands.

I was shown walking along the rim of the fell, with the

broad valley of the Ure beyond. The accent was on space and the words matched it well, for I had been mentioning the vast areas of little-known country that lie between the well-known dales. On the day it was filmed, the landscape had reached saturation point after weeks of above-average rainfall. Water glinted in the hollows and where there was a seepage through the beds of rushes.

Ian, the director, made the quite reasonable request that I might climb a wall (in a substantial place, of course) and stroll in that magnificent setting. I regretted leaving my wellingtons at home when I landed ankle deep in a brown soupy mixture. Later, while negotiating a partly flooded gateway with a farmer (who had wellies), I was splashed up to the knees. Hopefully, I would not be asked to swim Semerwater.

The farmer, Matthew Bell, had waited patiently in his Land-Rover, at the end of the queue of vehicles, as the filming took place. Now he came into his own, agreeing to allow his work with sheep to be filmed.

He opened the gate wide and sent the dog on an out-run. His whistles passed on his instructions in a clear, unemotional way. For a time the dog was out of sight; then a movement among the sheep indicated its position. It was a moderately old dog, 'past its best', but keen. A centuries-old routine was enacted under the gaze of Brian's hand-held camera, for sheep are too quick for a man to gather them unaided. Sheep farming, a major occupation on the Pennines, is possible only because there is, in the collie, a means of gathering sheep on the uplands. A collie is the Artful Dodger of the Yorkshire skyline.

When the sheep had been moved, the mud-splashed dog rested. I asked Mr Bell if I might photograph him and the dog for *The Dalesman*. He readily agreed. Would he kindly ask the dog to sit on the capstone of a nearby wall? He would. And he did—while the television camera photographed me photographing them. Afterwards Brian said that although his experience of ciné-photography was long and varied, he would never forget one moment in that day's work—the look in the eyes of the dog as it wondered what on earth it was doing on top of a wall!

We called on Marie Hartley and Joan Ingilby, who have contributed to *The Dalesman* since the earliest days. Their home, Coleshouse at Askrigg, has been commended to lovers of the Dales in a book dealing with its acquisition and renovation. We were invited into their workroom—a quiet place, brightly adorned with some of Marie's paintings of the locality.

For a time we pondered on the early days of *The Dalesman* and letters received in 1939 from Harry J. Scott, inviting them to contribute. They did—at 'a guinea a time' (the all-purpose fee for quite a few years). In those days, Marie Hartley's companion in the Dales was Ella Pontefract; they used a caravan as a base while collecting material for the first of many books—a study of Swaledale, published in 1934. Miss Pontefract died in 1945, aged only 48 years, and Joan Ingilby took her place in their long-term studies of Dales life and traditions. This work led to many books, including one on the old handknitters of the Dales, which Harry Scott commissioned.

To own a country cottage and live by writing about the countryside and its people is an attractive idea—the sort of which dreams are made. Many people have tried it: most have failed, wrongly believing that such a life can be an extended holiday in pleasant surroundings. Sustained writing is hard work, both mentally and physically. It is attended by bodily aches and prickling eyes. When a book takes over, there is little time for anything else, even for preparing meals. The partners in this enterprise, however, allow themselves time in the afternoon for a walk.

Theirs has been a true collaboration: they write a chapter each, then exchange the chapters for criticism and revision. 'I am best at the broad sweep of a book,' Marie Hartley once told me. 'Joan is a stickler for detail. We accept each other's criticism in the right spirit; we work in perfect harmony.'

For an hour, the presence of a television team was cheerfully accepted. A room that was usually quiet now

buzzed with technical talk. The light from arc lamps pried
into what were usually shadowy corners; wires were taped
to carpets. I looked through a latticework of tripods and
metal stands. Light values were assessed, sound levels
tested. I was asked not to converse with our principal subjects for fear of robbing the televised talk of its spontaneity.
The camera 'panned' over an oil painting of Askrigg; it
scanned an array of books written by the collaborators,
and it shamelessly noted the contents of private letters.

Alan Bennett, the playwright, had agreed to appear in
the film and to give the commentary. He knew *The Dalesman*
and confessed, with a cheeky Yorkshire smile, that he did
not buy it—copies were given to him. We walked and
talked about vernacular architecture, about the joys of
mushrooming and about Yorkshire humour.

He reminded us of a story that had appeared in *The
Dalesman*. A visitor to London dodged people and traffic
and eventually found himself on a traffic island with a
policeman. They engaged in polite conversation. The
policeman remarked that it was busy in London that day.
Said the visitor, who came from Yorkshire, 'Yes—there's a
trip in from Dent' (a village of about 200 souls).

Inevitably, we went to see the Hodgsons of New Ing. Our
little convoy headed southwards from Clapham in thicken-
ing mist, and eventually it was so thick we could almost
taste it. I led the way along the rutted lane leading to the
farm. We stopped to do some filming. So dense was the fog
we ran the risk of losing contact with the vehicles. I knew
that in minutes the unhappy faces would have brightened
in the presence of Arthur and Doreen, not forgetting the
dog and Arthur's collection of carved sticks, otherwise
known as shepherds' crooks. He had unbridled his im-
agination and turned out carvings of a whole range of
creatures, not just the customary dog or sheep. One stick
held a sculpture of man, dog and sheep. He had even
carved out his name in solid horn!

It was as I thought. Spirits rose in Arthur's breezy
company. Bodies chilled by mist as chilling and damp as a

dish-cloth responded to light and warmth. Ian and Brian, working in their metal thicket, with the many wires extending like a root system, captured on film pictures of Arthur filing sheep horn while his sheepdog lay playfully on its back at his feet. Ian had told me that the ratio of film exposed to film used is around eight to one, so high selectivity would be necessary, especially as this was a film about *The Dalesman* and Arthur—like Alan Bennett—had to be given the chance to tell viewers that he received a free copy of the magazine, from me!

I asked Arthur about the sika deer and mentioned Nan, who was quite often in her later life roused from her seat by the fire and taken across the farm when something interested had happened, such as when a deer calf was born, or one memorable night in haytime when the last cart was being led to the barn by the light of a full moon. Arthur updated the Gothic horror story. After telling us about the 'presence' in the house, of mysterious footfalls and a 'something' in the lane, he mentioned the place where an apparition had been seen and added that a few nights before, when some visitors were approaching the farmhouse, their new car had a complete electrical failure at that precise spot. It was excellent television.

Towards the end of the week, the curtains of cloud parted to reveal all with clarity and colour. We filmed the 'girls' packing copies of the magazine. I took part in a sequence (which was not used) in which I had to drive my car along the top road from Clapham as the mist capitulated to the sun. I remembered this because my companion, resting on the spare front seat, was a walkie-talkie radio set which spoke to me when any directions had to be given. Could it have been a foretaste of things to come?

With mounting excitement, we filmed autumn-tinted leaves in the village and headed for Arthur's farm through a technicoloured world. It was sunny in the lane. Shadows were visibly shrinking in the deer croft. Arthur and Doreen were at home. He walked into the croft with a bucket containing food and shouted. A few yards away, the camera was 'turning' and the microphone was alive at the end of its long boom. The sika deer arrived: they were in their winter coat of rich brown. The big stag was showing more than usual interest in a hind, which was more interested in food than procreation. The stag was licking its nostrils, to improve its scenting capability. The tongue flicked in and out of its mouth. When stag and hind were some four yards from the camera, the inevitable happened: the stag mounted the hind. A penis gleamed in the autumn daylight. That particular piece of film was not used but I hope it did not end up on the legendary cutting-room floor. It was probably the best film ever taken of sika deer mating.

Autumn seemed a good time to reflect and to introduce the new Editor of *The Dalesman*, David Joy, at his home at Hebden in Wharfedale. We were shown conversing with Geoff Lund, the waller, who—I discovered—is a son of Mowdy Bill Lund, the mole-catcher in Littondale, one of the first dalesmen I interviewed when I began work with the magazine. We heard of the privation of life in a big family when the income was slight, of meals composed of 'porridge and mouse muck' and of the days when a brother came home with swan eggs, which made 'lovely custards'.

The film ended where it began—on that old green lane near Bainbridge. I reflected on the inevitability of change. Forty years—my time with *The Dalesman*—were just a blink in the story of the Dales. Many changes have taken place and will continue to take place. It is all part of the natural process. There was time, in the closing seconds of the film, just before the 'credits' appeared on the screen, to compare *The Dalesman* to a river and to hope that, like a river, it would be unstoppable . . .

All Futura Books are available at your bookshop or newsagent, or can be ordered from the following address: Futura Books, Cash Sales Department, P.O. Box 11, Falmouth, Cornwall TR10 9EN.

Please send cheque or postal order (no currency), and allow 60p for postage and packing for the first book plus 25p for the second book and 15p for each additional book ordered up to a maximum charge of £1.90 in U.K.

B.F.P.O. customers please allow 60p for the first book, 25p for the second book plus 15p per copy for the next 7 books, thereafter 9p per book

Overseas customers, including Eire, please allow £1.25 for postage and packing for the first book, 75p for the second book and 28p for each subsequent title ordered.